HEROES OF HISTORY

JOHN ADAMS

Independence Forever

HEROES OF HISTORY

JOHN ADAMS

Independence Forever

JANET & GEOFF BENGE

Emerald Books
P.O. BOX 635, LYNNWOOD, WA 98046

Emerald Books are distributed through YWAM Publishing. For a full list of titles, including other great biographies, visit our website at www.ywampublishing.com or call 1-800-922-2143.

John Adams: Independence Forever

Published by Emerald Books
P.O. Box 635
Lynnwood, Washington 98046

Library of Congress Cataloging-in-Publication Data
Benge, Janet, 1958-
John Adams : independence forever / by Janet and Geoff Benge.
p. cm. -- (Heroes of history)
Includes bibliographical references.
ISBN-10: 1-883002-51-6
ISBN-13: 978-1-883002-51-0
1. Adams, John, 1735-1826--Juvenile literature. 2. Presidents--United
States--Biography--Juvenile literature. [1. Adams, John, 1735–1826. 2.
Presidents.] I. Benge, Geoff, 1954- II. Title.
E322 .B46 2002
973.4'4'092--dc21 2002012947

Fifth printing 2025

Printed in the United States of America

HEROES OF HISTORY

Abraham Lincoln
Alan Shepard
Ben Carson
Benjamin Franklin
Benjamin Rush
Billy Graham
Captain John Smith
Christopher Columbus
Clara Barton
Davy Crockett
Daniel Boone
Douglas MacArthur
Dwight Eisenhower
Elizabeth Fry
Ernest Shackleton
Frederick Douglass
George Washington
George Washington Carver
Harriet Tubman
John Adams
Laura Ingalls Wilder
Louis Zamperini
Meriwether Lewis
Milton Hershey
Orville Wright
Ronald Reagan
Theodore Roosevelt
Thomas Edison
William Bradford
William Penn
William Wilberforce
Winston Churhill

Available in paperback, e-book, and audiobook formats.
Curriculum Guides are available for all of the U.S. biographies.
www.Heroesofhistory.com

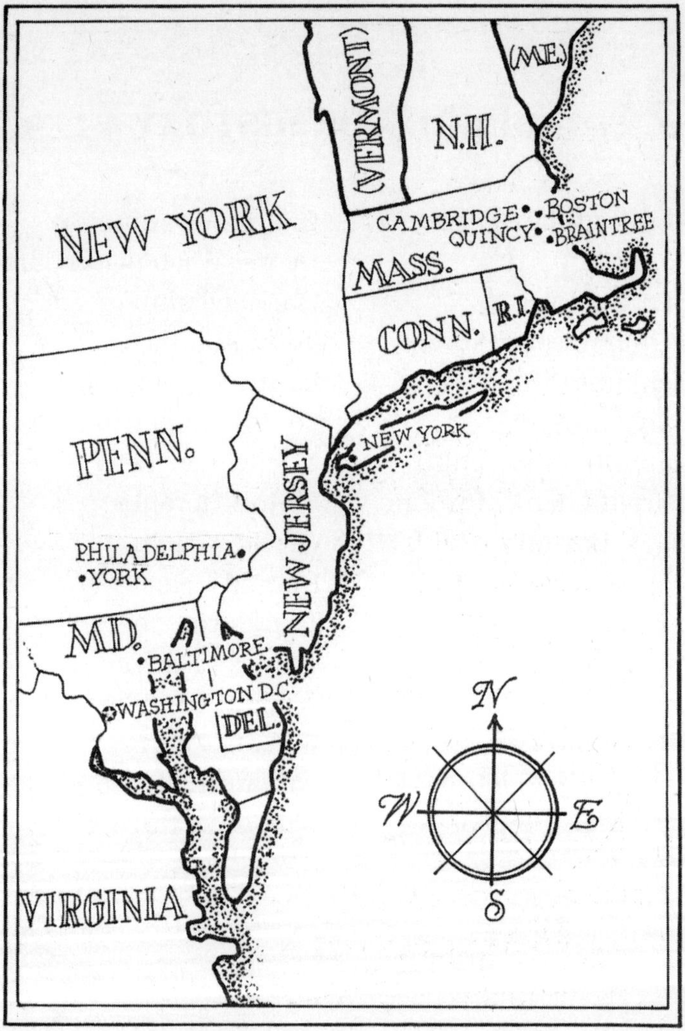

(VERMONT)
(ME.)
N.H.
NEW YORK
CAMBRIDGE
BOSTON
QUINCY
BRAINTREE
MASS.
R.I.
CONN.
PENN.
NEW YORK
NEW JERSEY
PHILADELPHIA
YORK
MD.
BALTIMORE
WASHINGTON D.C.
DEL.
VIRGINIA
N
W
E
S

Contents

Chapter 1

Traitor

John Adams looked up at the billowing sails of the *Boston*. "Let out the mainsail!" he heard Captain Tucker yell. Four sailors rushed past him and scaled the mast, where they adjusted the ropes. They worked quickly, ready for the captain's next order.

The *Boston* picked up speed as it plowed through the frigid waters of the Atlantic Ocean. John turned and headed for the stern of the ship. His heart sank as he looked behind them: The British man-of-war was still in hot pursuit. He reached for his eyeglass and peered at the other ship's deck. Sure enough, the sailors on the vessel were also trimming their sails to catch the extra gusts of wind. It had been this way, with the man-of-war on their tail, for two long days now, and John wondered what was finally going to break the deadlock between them.

John stepped back and stared at the leather trunk lashed to the deck. He checked the knots that held it there. Suddenly he heard a voice behind him. "Papa, what's in there, and why did you bring it on deck?"

It was John's eleven-year-old son Johnny. John looked at the boy and carefully chose his words so as not to alarm him. "All of the official papers I brought with me are in there," he said in a level voice. "If the ship that's giving chase catches us, I am going to cut the rope that binds the trunk to the deck and push it overboard. It's very heavy. I've put some cast iron in it so it will sink right away."

"But they won't catch us, will they?" Johnny asked.

John would have liked to assure his son, but there was no point in hiding the truth. "I wish I knew," he said, patting the boy on the shoulder. "Only time will tell. But you must promise me one thing. No matter what happens, you have to be brave and do whatever Captain Tucker tells you. Do you understand?"

Johnny looked up, bewildered. "But I'll be with you, Papa. You and I will be together, and you can tell me what to do."

"I hope so," John said looking away. "But just in case we get separated, you do exactly as the captain tells you."

Johnny gulped back a tear. "Yes, Papa. I promise."

"Now go below and finish your translation work. We can't allow a little thing like a man-of-war to stop your studies, can we?"

Johnny grinned and headed below deck, but John stayed watching the ship behind them. He wished he could have told his son the whole truth, but it would have terrified the boy. The part about throwing the trunk overboard was true, but if the British did overrun the ship, John intended to follow the trunk to the bottom of the ocean.

It's not that he wanted to, but he couldn't see a better option.

In the eyes of the king of England, he was a traitor. Not only had he advocated declaring independence for the American colonies from Great Britain, he had voted for it and proudly affixed his signature to the Declaration of Independence. If he were captured by the British, he would be taken back to England and hanged.

Gazing over the stern of the *Boston*, John could see the British man-of-war still in pursuit. *How ironic,* he thought as he wiped sea spray off his eyeglass. *All my life I have been a loyal British subject, a citizen of the Massachusetts colony, and now the British would gladly execute me if they got the chance."*

John frowned. How could he possibly explain this complicated situation to his oldest son? By comparison John's childhood had been very ordinary. His own father had been involved in politics, but that profession had never led to anything as dangerous as the moment in which John now found himself. As a boy growing up in Massachusetts, John never imagined that politics could lead to the peril he now faced on the open seas.

Chapter 2

It's a Farmer You Want to Be, Is It?

John Adams! Are you listening to me?" Master Cleverly barked as he rapped his stick on the desk.

John whipped his head around to face the front of the classroom. "Yes, sir," he replied, though he had no idea where the class was in the Latin textbook.

"I hope so!" the teacher continued. "Your father pays hard-earned money for you to be here. You should be taking advantage of the opportunity."

John nodded and redirected his attention to *Lily's Latin Grammar*, but inside he groaned. How many times had he been told that he should take advantage of the opportunity to go to Latin school? Every other day, he guessed. He was thirteen years old, and by now most of his friends in Braintree had left school and were helping their fathers on their family farms. *But not me,* John thought glumly. *I'm not that lucky. I get to stay at school until I master all of this text, and then what reward do I get? More school. When will it end?*

It was a good question, and one that John, as the oldest boy in his family, already knew the answer to. He had two younger brothers, ten-year-old Peter and four-year-old Elihu, and although they all looked alike, with curly blond hair and bright blue eyes, the two younger boys were destined for a life totally different from John's. They would not have to endure all this learning. Like John, Peter had gone to a dame school, where classes were held in the home of a female teacher, to learn the basics of reading, writing, and arithmetic. But by now he had already left school and had started working on the farm. Like so many families in Massachusetts, John's parents, John and Susanna Adams, were determined that their oldest son should get the best education possible.

A bell broke John's concentration. Much to his relief, it was recess time. Outside, the morning fog that had rolled in from Massachusetts Bay had lifted and the leaves on the oak trees that surrounded Master Cleverly's house were a blaze of vivid oranges and reds. As John jumped down the steps and into the yard, the autumn colors reminded him that it was the time for wild geese to be heading south. That, in turn, led him to start thinking about his favorite pastime—hunting.

Suddenly John could almost feel the weight of his rifle in his hands and the smooth action of the bolt. He looked around. The other boys were beginning an informal wrestling match, while Master Cleverly, whom John thought was one of the laziest teachers around, was inside the house. John's heart beat fast; now was the perfect time to make his getaway!

John crept slowly around the side of the clapboard house and out of sight of the other boys. Then he burst into a run. How good it was to be free from school! There would be no more Latin or astronomy for him today. John ran all the way down the road, past the blacksmith's shop and the gristmill, until he got close to his own house. Then, keeping a careful eye out for his mother, he made his way around the seventy-year-old clapboard house to his bedroom, a low, steep-roofed lean-to at the back of the house. John had crept home for his gun many times before, and he was proud of the fact that he had never been caught doing so. He slipped the bolt on the door and reached his hand inside to get his rifle and powder pouch.

With these items safely in hand, John skirted around the stone wall that marked the edge of the family farm. It was two farms, actually. The farm with the house the Adams family lived in consisted of six acres of orchards and arable land. Four years before, John's father had also bought the nine-and-one-half-acre farm next door. It had a house identical to the Adamses' on it. In fact, the two houses sat side by side about ten feet apart. The second house was rented to John's cousin Ann and her husband, Dr. Elisha Savil. John's father had joined the two properties together and called them Penn's Hill Farm.

John headed up Penn's Hill. When he reached the top, he sat down for a minute to catch his breath and admire the view. There was so much to see from there. About twelve miles to the north lay the colonial capital of Boston, and John could clearly make out the lighthouse in Boston Harbor. To the east was the deep-blue water of the Atlantic Ocean, which stretched as far as he could see.

As John sat there, he imagined his ancestors sailing across the Atlantic Ocean from England to Plymouth, twenty-five miles to the south of Braintree. He was proud of his ancestors. It was 1749 now, but more than 120 years before, in December 1620, his great-great-grandfather, John Alden, had been the first man to step off the *Mayflower* onto the American continent. Eighteen years later another great-great-grandfather arrived in the colony. His name was Henry Adams, and he, with his wife, Edith, and their eight sons and one daughter, had joined a Puritan party emigrating from Somersetshire, England. The families had become some of the first settlers in Braintree. John had always thought Braintree was a strange name, until his father explained to him that the village was named after a town in England from where some of the early settlers had come.

John stood up and buttoned his jacket against the chill in the air. The long New England winter was definitely on its way. He strolled down the hill, his rifle slung over his shoulder, and headed in the direction of the Neponset River. He had a favorite spot there, where the migrating birds often stopped to rest and feed.

No great flocks of geese arrived that afternoon, but John did not care too much. Just being outside, with the drone of insects and the smell of hay, brightened his spirits.

The sun was well past its zenith when John decided that he had better be heading home. If he waited any longer, school would be long over and his mother might ask questions about where he had been. He walked fast to keep warm, and once again he slipped around the side of the house so that he could put his rifle away before he went boldly in the front door. Just as he rounded the corner of the house, John froze. There was his father, pitchfork in hand and walking straight toward him!

John thought quickly. It was best to carry on as if he had not skipped school. Above all, he must not look guilty. He forced himself to smile as naturally as he could. "Hello, Father," he said. "May I help you in the garden before dinner, or would you rather I milked the cow for Mother?"

The older John Adams looked down at his son. His voice was smooth but firm. "I would rather you told me the truth about what you're doing with your hunting rifle," he said.

John gulped. He had a decision to make. Either he could lie about where he had been and risk his father's finding out and being furious with him, or he could come clean and tell the truth and take whatever punishment he was given.

John looked at his father for a long moment. John's father was not a young man, like most of his friends' fathers. In fact he had married in his early forties and was now fifty-seven years old. But he still had a strong right arm—strong enough to give John a good whipping.

Before he lost his courage, John opened his mouth. "I skipped school," he said. "I already knew the lesson, so I went hunting on the marsh."

A long silence seemed to John to stretch on forever. Finally his father spoke. "I see. So how do you expect to get to Harvard if you will not apply yourself to your studies?"

John looked up at his father, who did not look angry as he normally did when he discovered John doing something wrong. This time he looked worn, and this change emboldened John. He spoke up. "You don't understand, Father. I do not want to go to Harvard. When I grow up, I want to be a farmer just like you, and I wish I could begin now. I've had enough school to last me a lifetime."

"You have, have you?" the elder Adams said, raising his eyebrows. "It's a farmer you want to be, is it?"

John nodded.

"Well, we'll see about that. Go and milk the cow now, and tomorrow you can begin your new life as a farmer. It's not all you think it might be."

"Yes, sir," John mumbled, hardly knowing what to think. Did his father mean he did not have to go back to Master Cleverly's school ever again? Were the plans for sending him to college—the thing he dreaded most—now forgotten? He did not know, but he was pleased that he did not have to go to school the next day.

As soon as the sun was up, John and his father ate breakfast and headed out into the damp morning. John Adams senior led the way past the garden shed, where he picked up two scythes. He handed one to his son. "Here, take this, and I'll show you what it is to be a farmer."

An hour later father and son stood side by side in knee-deep mud, slashing at the swamp grass. When they had cut down an armful, they added it to the pile they were making. The grass would be used to thatch the roofs on one of the farm's outbuildings, either the stable or the garden shed. The house itself was roofed with long split shingles to avoid the roof's catching fire from the sparks that floated up the chimney.

For the most part, John and his father worked in silence, which suited John just fine. Even though his back ached from bending over, he enjoyed the rhythm of bending and slashing. As he worked, his mind could wander, a risky practice at school. He thought of his future. Being a farmer was a wonderful idea. He had no desire to go to Cambridge, where Harvard University was located, or any other town, for that matter. He had been to Boston only twice in his entire life and found it a confusing and frustrating place to find his way around.

As he worked, John stole a look at his father. *My father has exactly the life I want to lead,* he thought. *He knows everything that's going on in*

Braintree; he is a church deacon, a lieutenant in the militia, and the selectman who practically runs the town's business. He owns his land and has as much to say at the town meetings as anyone else. And he never went to Latin school!

Father and son stopped for lunch, which consisted of mutton, cheese, and buttermilk biscuits. Then it was back to work, cutting thatch until dusk. John walked home beside his father, wondering what they would do tomorrow—thatch a roof, perhaps, or repair the stone wall around his mother's kitchen garden.

As they cleaned their scythes, John's father turned to him. "So how do you like farming now?" he asked.

John smiled. "I like it very well," he replied.

John watched as his father's face turned as dark as the mud on his boots. "Well, I *don't* like it so well," his father said. "You know I have set my heart on your going to college to get an education. Why are you so set against it?"

John took a deep breath. He knew it was either now or never to speak up. "It's not that I don't want to learn," he began. "It's that I don't like my schoolmaster. He is so lazy and cross that I will never be able to learn anything from him. If I could change schools and be taught by Master Marsh, I'll do my best to prepare for college."

"Ummm," his father replied. "Bring in some wood for the fire."

Later that night as John lay in bed beside his brother Peter, he boiled with anger. Why should the fact that he was the oldest son make him so different from his two brothers? Why couldn't one of them endure the torture of school and let him go free in the fields?

But for all his questions, John knew that nothing could change his father's mind, and he knew why. His father had been the second son in the family, and his older brother, Joseph Adams, was the one who had gone to college at Harvard while he had been forced to leave school and help his father on the farm at an early age. Uncle Joseph was now a prosperous minister in New Hampshire. John's father loved books and learning and always regretted that his brother, and not he, had been the one to get an education. He could not imagine someone wanting to give up the chance to go to school. Now that he had the opportunity to educate his son, he would not let the opportunity slip by, no matter how much John protested.

It's not fair, John thought, as tears dripped down his cheeks and onto his pillow. But the issue wasn't about fairness; it was about doing what his father told him to. So the following morning John dressed in his breeches and shirt, ready for another day at school. As John sat down to eat breakfast, his father smiled at him. "John, I have spoken to Master Marsh and persuaded him to take you. You will begin school there today. It is going to cost me a lot more money to send you there, so you had better apply yourself to your work. Do you understand?"

"Yes, sir, thank you," John replied. He could hardly believe his good fortune. "I will work hard and be ready for college as soon as I can."

Master Marsh, who ran a private boarding and day school for boys from his house, did prove to be a much better teacher than Master Cleverly, and just as he had promised, John worked hard for his new teacher. And although he still stared out the window sometimes, he resisted the urge to skip class.

Eighteen months later, Master Marsh informed John that he thought he was ready for the Examination of Candidates for Admission to Harvard. It sounded like a very scary process to John, who had to go before a board made up of the president and tutors from the university and answer their questions. Then he had to take a test, which included translating a text from English into Latin.

It was a cool morning in late summer 1751 when fifteen-year-old John saddled up his horse for the ride to Cambridge. He was nervous but not nearly as nervous as he would have been if Master Marsh had not offered to go with him.

John's entire family gathered outside the stable to see him off.

"Come back with good news," his father said, clapping him on the back. "Remember, you have a proud tradition to keep up. Your Uncle Joseph graduated from Harvard in 1710."

John tried to smile despite the somersaults going on in his stomach. He did not need to be reminded that his uncle was a graduate of the college!

"Bring me back a present," yelled six-year-old Elihu.

John waved good-bye to them all and rode the half mile to Master Marsh's house. He tied up his horse and knocked at the door. A servant answered. "Master Marsh will not be going anywhere today," she said matter-of-factly. "He has the worst cold I've ever seen, and he's all tucked up in bed with a bottle of my special lemon-honey elixir."

John's heart dropped. "But..."

"Sorry, Master John," she said, starting to shut the door. "I doubt if he will be on his feet for a week or so."

John walked slowly back to his horse, wondering what he should do. As he stared back down the road he could see the smoke rising from the chimney at his house. His parents and brothers would be inside talking and laughing. He desperately wanted to be back there. All he had to do was turn around and tell his father that he could not go to the examination on his own. *But,* John thought, *how can I disappoint him like that? He has already given up so much so that I could go to Master Marsh's school.*

John dug his heels into the sides of his horse. The animal broke into a gallop, and horse and rider headed north. *I have an appointment at noon,* John told himself. *Somehow I have to get through this alone.*

Chapter 3

Congratulations, Master Adams

It was midday when John slowed his horse to a trot outside the walls of Harvard College. In front of him stood three imposing four-stories-high red-brick buildings set in a horseshoe shape around a large square. John recalled Master Marsh's telling him that the building on the left was called Massachusetts Hall and that was where the president's office was located.

As his horse trotted along the outside of the wall, John fought the urge to turn around and head back home to everything that was familiar to him. Instead he dismounted at the gate and led his horse around to the back of the buildings, where he guessed he would find a stable. Sure enough, one was there, and he hitched his horse before walking slowly toward the main doors of

Massachusetts Hall. As he walked, he tried reciting some Latin grammar rules to himself, but he was so nervous he could barely recall a word of them.

Ten minutes later, John found himself sitting on a straight-backed wooden chair staring at four men. The men all wore long, curly white wigs and long black gowns. And none of them seemed to know how to smile.

"I am President Holyoake," said an old man with a double chin. "And you, I take it, are John Adams of Braintree."

"Yes, sir," John stammered, wishing more than ever that his tutor were there with him.

"And I am Tutor Mayhew," the second man said. "Tell us, John, what are your favorite subjects in school?"

John desperately wanted to say that he did not have any favorite subjects, that this whole interview was a huge mistake, and that all he really wanted was to be a farmer like his father, but he dared not. Instead he replied, "Mathematics, sir. I find myself quite enjoying mathematics."

"Good, good," Tutor Mayhew replied, smiling for the first time. "And how is your Latin?"

John smiled back. "I have worked very hard with my schoolmaster."

Tutor Mayhew pushed two pieces of paper across the table toward John and said, "Here is a passage in English. Would you please translate it into Latin. I'll get you a quill."

John's stomach lurched as he glanced at the passage. It was far harder than anything he had ever attempted. He wondered whether he should stay and make a fool of himself trying to translate it or just thank the men for their time and walk out now. In the end his knees felt too weak to stand, so he stayed where he was.

His hand shook as he picked up the quill. Suddenly Tutor Mayhew broke the silence. "I can see you are feeling a little pressured," he said. "No doubt the result of a long, hard ride so early in the morning. We have another student arriving soon, so why don't you come with me, and you can do the translation in my office. It might suit you better to be alone."

John breathed a sigh of relief. Away from these four sets of prying eyes, he might be able to think better. He gathered up his things and followed Tutor Mayhew down a long, wood-paneled corridor and into a sunny office.

"There, I think this will serve you much better," the tutor exclaimed. "There is no need to be nervous." He pulled some books from his shelf and set them down beside John. "Here is a Latin dictionary and a grammar. You can use them to help you with your work," he said, patting John on the back. "And take as much time as you need. There is no hurry. I need to go back to the president. Can you find your way to me when you are finished?"

"Yes, sir," John replied. "And thank you."

"Oh, it is nothing," Tutor Mayhew said, waving his hand. "I still remember how nervous I was in my college interview. Just take a deep breath and get to work." He walked out and shut the door quietly behind him.

John sat for a long moment, glad that he could work alone. Then he plunged into the translation, and much to his surprise, it was not nearly as difficult as it had first looked.

When he was satisfied that he had done the best he could, John waited for the ink to dry and then delivered the paper to the four-man panel. Each man read it quickly, wrote a note at the bottom of the page, and passed it on to the next man to read. President Holyoake was the last to read it. When he was finished, he stood up and extended his hand to John. "Congratulations, Master Adams." he said. "You are accepted for admittance in the fall."

John stood up and hastily shook the president's hand. He could scarcely believe it. He was going to be attending Harvard College!

The journey home seemed so much shorter than the trip there, and John could hardly wait to tell his father the good news. He arrived back in Braintree just before dark, and news of his acceptance into Harvard spread rapidly throughout the small village.

John had only a few weeks of summer left before setting out for college, and he made the most of his time. He walked the Great Blue Hills behind Penn's Hill Farm and hunted for squirrels and raccoons. He swam in the river with his school friends and let his younger brother win all of his marbles from him. Then, as the nights began to get longer, John packed his few belongings and set off for Cambridge.

This time his father went with him, and they traveled in a gig. Sometimes they talked as they traveled, but most of the time they just sat in silence, listening to the rhythmic clip-clop of the horse's hooves on the baked earth. John thought about how much this all meant to his father. He knew his father had broken his own rule about never selling family land when he sold ten acres of his best farmland to pay for John's tuition. There was no question in John's mind how much his father wanted him to succeed, but there was another question that he did not want to think about. Just how much did he really want to succeed for himself and not for his family? John hated to admit it, but he still disliked reading and studying. And although his father expected him to become a minister after college, John was not sure that was what he wanted. He could not imagine himself spending hours visiting sick people or listening to people's problems. Nor could he imagine himself arguing over tiny shades of theological meaning. He did believe in God—he knew that much—but that did not mean that he wanted to spend the rest of his life preparing sermons and visiting the members of his congregation.

All of this led to the question John did not want to face: If he was not going to be a minister, what did he want to do after college? As he had done so many times that summer, John tried to put the question out of his mind. After all, he had four years at Harvard before he had to decide.

When they arrived at the college, John was introduced to his new roommates, Joseph Stockbridge and Thomas Sparhawk. Together the three boys moved into their room on the ground floor at the northwest corner of Massachusetts Hall. The room was plain and sparsely furnished, and the boys soon found out they had little time to do anything else in the room but study and sleep.

The morning after John arrived, the college routine began. The ninety young men who made up the Harvard student body were roused by a bell at 5:30 A.M. They were expected to be dressed and assembled for prayer in Holden Chapel by 6:00 A.M. Following the chapel service, breakfast was served at seven. On the first morning, John forgot to bring his knife, fork, and spoon with him and had to run back to his room to get them. He was surprised to find that no one washed his cutlery when the meal was over. It was a Harvard tradition to wipe the cutlery clean on the tablecloth.

After breakfast President Holyoake gathered the freshmen students together and officially welcomed them. He told the boys what a privilege it was to be studying at the oldest college on the American continent. A Puritan minister named John Harvard, he said, had founded the college back in 1636. He had donated half of his estate to the college, along with his vast library. Now, in 1751, the president of the college went on to explain that only one out of every two hundred New England men got to go to college (and no women, of course), so it was up to the boys to give their very best. It was assumed that once their four years of study at the college were over, most of them would go on to one of four careers. Some would become ministers and others teachers, both of which were professions a student could enter straightaway. Other students would choose to become lawyers and doctors, which required the graduate to apprentice himself to an established lawyer or doctor for several years' more study.

John listened carefully to all President Holyoake had to say. He was quite sure he did not want to be a minister, and he didn't have enough patience to be a teacher. And since the sight of human blood made him squeamish, being a doctor was not likely either. That left being a lawyer, which was one profession John knew his parents would hate to see him pursue. Most New England farmers, including his father, despised lawyers as self-serving and without moral compass. John would have to think long and hard about what he wanted to do once he finished his time at college.

After the welcome speech was over, the freshmen all went to a Greek class, where they stayed until a bell announced it was lunchtime. After lunch students studied until five o'clock, when they had another round of prayers, followed by dinner. They then had study time until all candles were snuffed out at nine o'clock.

This routine remained the same five days a week, except that the morning class alternated between studying Greek, Latin, physics, logic, and rhetoric (which taught the boys the art of public speaking and concise writing). The monotony was broken on Saturday, when the entire student body spent the day studying theology with President Holyoake. On Sundays the students were expected to attend two long church services in the college chapel.

At first John felt constrained by all the bells, compulsory meetings, and rules. It seemed there was a rule for everything. If a student broke the Sabbath, played cards, went skating without permission, picked a lock, slept during prayers, left the grounds without a note from his tutor, or kept a gun in his room, he was fined ten shillings for each offense.

John dared not write home for money to pay fines, so he soon settled down to a life of study, reading, and discussion. And the thing that began to surprise him as he did so was how much he began to enjoy these activities. He spent more and more time in the library reading the classics and copying chapters of books into notebooks so that he could refer to them later. He especially loved reading Cicero, the great Roman orator, and memorized many of his speeches.

Once John settled into his studies, time flew by. He looked forward to returning to Braintree at the end of every semester, and although he still loved to wander in the hills and along the shoreline, his horizons were wider now, and he knew he would not be content to be a farmer after all.

Still, as his four years of college passed, one question continued to plague John: What would he do when he graduated? He still had not answered the question by the time his graduation rolled around in May 1755, though he tried not to let the problem prevent him from enjoying the festivities.

It was a great celebration. His whole family, including his Boylston and Adams cousins, came to see him graduate, as did many friends from Braintree. The graduation involved a week-long carnival that drew peddlers, minstrels, and circus acts from miles around.

In the commencement program for the graduating class, each student was ranked two ways. First, students were ranked in order of importance according to the family line they came from. The sons of rich and influential families were ranked at the top, and those with little social standing at the bottom. Here John was ranked fourteenth out of twenty-five graduating students. His middle standing came from his Boylston relatives on his mother's side and the fact that his father was a deacon. The second ranking was based upon the students' academic performance. Here John did much better. All of his reading and studying had paid off, and he graduated third in his class.

As a result of his academic achievement, John was asked to give a commencement speech. He chose to speak on the topic "Civil government is absolutely necessary for men." Thinking about and discussing politics was something that interested John. This led him to think that he might like to be a lawyer, though he dared not tell his father. As it happened, his career path opened as the result of his commencement speech.

When the graduation ceremony was over, a tall, gaunt man stepped up to John. "I must congratulate you on your speech, young man," he said. "It was one of the most clearly argued speeches I've heard in a long time."

"Thank you," John replied. "Where are you from?"

"I am sorry. I forgot to introduce myself. I am Thaddeus Maccarty, the minister from Worcester, and I must admit I am here on a mission. I have been sent to find a new teacher for our town's grammar school. I was wondering whether you are otherwise engaged yet, or would you be interested in the position?"

John's mind whirled. He did not really want to be a teacher, but if he didn't take the job, what would he do? Go home and live with his parents and try to withstand his father's constant prodding for him to become a minister. "That sounds very interesting. I have not been engaged for any other job yet. Tell me more," he said.

The two men spoke for several more minutes, at the end of which time John agreed to take the job. He would start his new career in less than a month. *It would make my parents happy, and I have to do something,* he told himself. But as he left Harvard College and journeyed back to Braintree with his family, John wondered whether he had done the right thing. Could he really settle into the life of a small-town teacher?

Chapter 4

A Career at Last

Three weeks later John was staring into the faces of forty-five boys and girls at the Worcester Latin School. He was not impressed with what he saw. In fact, that night when he returned to his new lodgings at the home of a man named Colonel Chandler, he put his thoughts down on paper. "I have charge of a large number of little runtlings, just capable of lisping A.B.C. and troubling the Master."

The dreary days dragged by as John tried to adjust to spending his time in a single, stuffy schoolroom filled with "little runtlings." He missed so many things about Harvard, especially the mental challenge of preparing speeches and debates and the camaraderie he'd had with his college friends. The only thing he liked about Worcester was that, although it was a small village of fifteen hundred people, it was the seat of the county government and court was often held there. Whenever he could, John liked to sit at the back of the courtroom and listen to the cases being heard. Most of them were such mundane affairs as thefts, drunken assaults, land claim disputes, and arguments over inheritances, but John found them much more interesting than anything that happened in the schoolhouse!

John was also fascinated with discussing politics with the local residents. The people were well informed about the newest round of fighting going on between the English and the French over land in the American colonies. John thought this was probably because they had experienced events of the war firsthand. Seven years earlier the Nipmuck Indians, with the backing of the French, had raided Worcester, making everyone pay attention to the squabbling that had been going on now for more than fifty years. At the heart of the fight was the question of who would rule America, the English or the French. These two European powers fought over fishing rights, land borders, and control of trade with the Indians. Most of the Indians resented the English for settling on their land and sided with the French.

By 1755, when John arrived in Worcester, things were becoming very tense. The French and Indian War (linked to the worldwide Seven Years War) was in full swing. The French had claimed Canada and were pushing south into the fertile Ohio Valley, where they had built Fort Duquesne. A young Virginian colonel named George Washington was doing his best to keep the French from advancing east, but no one was sure whether the English colonists were strong enough to resist the French troops and stop them from overrunning the colonies. At any opportunity John argued with people about how the English should handle the French and Indian problem.

During this time the town of Worcester hosted four thousand English troops led by Lord Jeffrey Amherst. The soldiers were on their way west to Fort William Henry on Lake George. They set up camp just outside Worcester, and the town's people invited them for meals and social evenings. John found his heart swelling with pride as he watched these redcoats marching in formation. He was glad to be an Englishman and to live under the British flag.

Most of John's time was not spent admiring the troops who marched through the town. Rather, he spent most of his time in the classroom or in his room preparing lessons. At times, to keep the boredom at bay, John would let his imagination ramble. He liked to think of the boys and girls in his charge as a minisociety. Once he explained it to his cousin in a letter:

> I sometimes, in my sprightly moments, consider myself, in my great chair at school, as some dictator at the head of a commonwealth. In this little state I can discover all the great geniuses, all the surprising actions and

> revolutions of the great world in miniature. I have several renowned generals but three feet high, and several deep-projecting politicians in petticoats. I have others catching and dissecting flies, accumulating remarkable pebbles, cockleshells, etc., with as ardent curiosity as any virtuoso in the Royal Society.

Observing the children in their serious and silly moments made school bearable for John, but as the end of the year approached, he realized he had to make some kind of move. He wrote in his journal, "I have no books, no time, no friends." John knew he had to make plans to get out of teaching before he became even more depressed with the whole business. Sitting in on the court sessions had helped settle the question of what he would do for a career. Twenty-year-old John Adams wanted to be a lawyer.

It was not easy breaking the news to his parents, who were not at all impressed with his choice. But after a year of doing something he hated, John knew it was important to find something he loved. And he was sure that that something was practicing law. In fact, John was not alone in wanting to pursue law as a career. Many young men from the colonies were thinking about becoming lawyers. This was a result of the ongoing French and Indian War. As the colonies raised their own militias, they created a lot of legal work, such as writing contracts and working out ways to legally import the materials they needed to keep the war going. Since lawyers were needed to do all this work, many new positions had to be filled by smart young men like John Adams.

During the year he had been in Worcester, John had formed his own ideas about what was going to happen between England, France, and the American colonies. He did not tell everyone his thoughts, because he knew they would seem remote and far-fetched to many people. But he did write to his cousin, explaining to him the way he viewed the situation:

> All that part of Creation that lies within our observation is liable to change.... If we look into history, we shall find some nations rising from contemptible beginnings and spreading their influence, until the whole globe is subjected to their ways....
>
> England immediately upon this began to increase (the particular and minute cause of which I am not historian enough to trace) in power and magnificence, and is now the greatest nation upon the globe.
>
> Soon after the Reformation a few people came over into the new world for conscience sake. Perhaps this (apparently) trivial incident may transfer the great seat of empire into America. It looks likely to me. For if we can remove the turbulent Gallics [the French], our people, according to the exactest computations, will in another century, become more

> numerous than England itself. Should this be the case, since we have (I may say) all the naval stores of the nation in our hands, it will be easy to obtain the mastery of the seas, and then the united force of all Europe will not be able to subdue us. The only way to keep us from setting up for ourselves is to disunite us.... Keep us in distinct colonies....
>
> Be not surprised that I am turned politician. The whole town is immersed in politics.

John was sure that one day the American colonies would become more powerful than England, their mother country, and become independent, unless the English managed to get the colonies to squabble so much among themselves that they could not agree on being one free country together.

These were the things John loved to think on as he set about becoming a lawyer. There were no law schools in the colonies, and since he could not afford to go to London to school, he chose the route most colonial law students took. He found a lawyer who was willing to take him on as an apprentice.

Of course this lawyer, a man named James Putnam, would require John to pay him. It cost one hundred pounds, and so John kept his job as a schoolteacher during the day to pay for his apprenticeship and room and board. At night and on the weekends, he read the law books James loaned him. And every Saturday James would quiz John about what he had read so far. It was not long before John was also copying deeds and wills, looking up precedents, preparing briefs, even arguing a few small court cases. The whole apprenticeship took two years. Although John seldom had a spare moment, he knew it was worth it. Slowly he was moving toward a career that he knew he would love.

In August 1758 James decided that John had learned enough about law to write him a letter of certification, stating that he was competent to become a licensed lawyer. John was overjoyed. Several of the leading men in Worcester urged him to stay in the village and start his own law firm, but John had other ideas. He saw the letter of certification as a way out. He did not want to practice law in a small town like Worcester any more than he wanted to teach school there. He had his mind on bigger things. He wanted to be an up-and-coming lawyer in a big city rather than eke out a living dealing with unimportant law cases in a small town.

John was smart enough to know that he would have to reach his goal in steps. Although he fully intended to practice law in Boston one day, for now he was happy to move back into his parents' house in Braintree. They had invited him to return home, and since Braintree had no lawyer, there would be some work for him to do. In his spare time, John planned to ride into Boston and begin acquainting himself with the Boston court.

As soon as he had his letter of certification in hand, John packed his few belongings and headed back to Braintree. As he sat in the coach on the way home, he realized that there was not much he would miss about the place that had been his home for the past three years. He was very relieved to be free from the schoolhouse. No longer would he have to spend every evening studying, and he looked forward to once again socializing and reading for pleasure.

It did not take John long to settle back into his hometown. It had been seven years since he set out to attend Harvard, but not much had changed in Braintree in that time. It was still a sleepy little village, where most of the men farmed in the summer and took up some craft to get them through the long winter months.

Since Braintree belonged to the Boston judicial district, before John could practice law there he had to be admitted to the bar in Boston. He went about winning admittance to the bar in his usual, methodical way. He wrote down the names of the four top lawyers in Boston: Jeremiah Gridley, Oxenbridge Thacher, Benjamin Prat, and James Otis Jr. He decided to visit each lawyer in that order.

As he rode to Boston on Thursday, September 29, 1758, John reminded himself not to hope for too much help from these men. After all, once he had been admitted to the bar, he would become their competition. John was pleasantly surprised, then, when his visit with Jeremiah Gridley went so well.

Jeremiah was dean of Boston's bar association, and he quizzed John thoroughly on his knowledge of law. When the questioning was over, he smiled at John and said, "That was quite a show. Congratulations. I have seldom interviewed a novice with as much depth of knowledge as you have displayed."

"Thank you, sir," John replied, hoping his face had not turned too flush with the praise. "I would be grateful for any advice you could give me."

"Umm," Jeremiah said, stroking his chin. "As far as I see it, a young man like you—how old did you say you were?"

"Twenty-two," John replied.

"Well, as I said, a young man like you needs only two pieces of advice. First," Jeremiah waved his arm around the room, "as you can see, I have built a prosperous business for myself, but it does not do to pursue the study of law to make money; pursue the law for its own sake, and the money will come." He paused for a moment before going on. "The second piece of advice is no easier to follow than the first, though just as vital. Don't marry too soon. Marriage takes a lot of time and money, and you will need both to get your career started."

"Thank you, sir," John said. "I appreciate your advice and will try my best to follow it."

Jeremiah clapped him on the back. "I have no doubt you will, my boy, and that you will go a long way. I would be glad to vote you onto the bar, and I think I can do more than that for you. As you can see, I have an extensive library of law books. Feel free to borrow them whenever you are in Boston."

John looked around the book-lined room. The chance to borrow any of these books was the best gift he could ever ask for. "Thank you," he stammered, hardly knowing how to express his gratitude. "I am greatly in your debt."

The two men continued to talk for a few minutes, and then they shook hands as John went off in search of the next lawyer he planned to call on—Oxenbridge Thacher.

The conversation with this man turned out to be quite different from the one John had enjoyed with Jeremiah Gridley. It appeared that Oxenbridge was not at all interested in what John knew about the law, and the two men chatted happily about many other topics, including the meaning of sin. Whatever they talked about, though, seemed to satisfy Oxenbridge that John was ready to be admitted to the bar, because he promised John his vote.

Everything was going better than John could have expected until he got to Benjamin Prat's office. Benjamin was a rather grumpy man who had lost a leg after a fall from a horse, and he looked as if he were in constant pain. He snapped at John for not bringing him a letter of introduction from James Putnam and refused to spend more than a minute with him. John was a little taken aback by this lawyer's curt manner, but he determined to keep going and visit the fourth man on his list, James Otis Jr.

Thankfully, James was a much more pleasant man than Benjamin Prat, and he welcomed John into his office and made him feel at ease from the beginning. This was no simple task, since John knew that James was one of the wealthiest men in Boston. James came from a prominent family, had married into an even richer one, and now owned many slaves and threw the most lavish balls in the district. Like Jeremiah Gridley, James asked John many questions about the law and then readily agreed to vote for him.

John left Boston a very satisfied man. He had three of the most influential lawyers in the colony behind him, and he felt sure he would be admitted to the bar soon, even without Benjamin Prat's help. Happily, he had gauged the situation correctly, and on November 6, 1758, John Adams was admitted to the bar in a ceremony before the superior court of Boston. He was a young man, eager to take on his first case, though he would have been less eager if he had known how embarrassing the entire incident would turn out to be.

Chapter 5

The Child Independence Was Born

John picked up his quill, dipped it into the ink pot, and carefully wrote the words *Lambert* v. *Field* at the top of the page. It was his first court case, and he was determined to argue it the best way he knew how, even though it was a fairly small matter. John was the lawyer for Joseph Field, a farmer in Braintree who had had some of his crops trampled by two of his neighbor's horses. The horses had broken down a fence to get in, and now Joseph's neighbor, Luke Lambert, was refusing to pay for the damage his horses had done. He argued that the horses had not been in the field long enough to do that much damage. However, there were witnesses who had seen Luke's horses enter Joseph's land and damage his crops. As far as John was concerned, it was a straightforward case that he would easily win.

As John prepared for the case, for the first time he drew up his own writ. In the past, when he had worked for James Putnam, a town clerk had been employed to draw up the writs. John wanted to prove that he was quite capable of doing all the legal paperwork himself. But legal papers had to be worded very precisely, and having no experience at writing writs, John made a regrettable and unnoticed error.

The case of *Lambert* v. *Field* was heard before Colonel Josiah Quincy, justice of the peace and the richest man in town. Rather unfairly, the colonel's son Samuel Quincy, who had just opened a law practice in Boston, was Luke Lambert's lawyer. When Colonel Quincy read the writ John had written, he threw out Joseph Field's claim because John had failed to include the phrase "the county in the direction to the constables of Braintree" in the description of the piece of land in question. John was devastated that his mistake had cost Joseph Field his case. Joseph Field was none too happy about the situation either. He ranted and railed against John in the local tavern, and soon everyone in Braintree knew the ins and outs of the case and how John Adams had managed to lose it. Even John's parents were angry with him, and John vowed never to make another mistake like that again.

After a few weeks the talk died down, and the townspeople found new events other than John and the lost court case to gossip about. John took on several other small legal cases that he won. He even became friends with Samuel Quincy and began seeing Samuel's coy sister, Hannah. Until this time John had not spent much time around young women, and he found Hannah to be delightful company. She laughed at all his jokes, and when she batted her blue eyes at him, he felt his heart thumping. John was sure he was in love, but there was a problem. He recalled Jeremiah Gridley's advice to him that if he wanted to make a name for himself as a lawyer, he should not marry young.

While John was trying to figure out what he should do about this, Hannah was becoming impatient. She turned her attention to one of John's fellow Harvard students, Bela Lincoln. Bela, a young doctor, was ready and willing to marry her right away, and before John knew it, the two were engaged and planning a large wedding.

This turn of events left John heartbroken. He could not even drink a cup of tea because doing so reminded him of the times he and Hannah had sat talking and drinking tea together. Lest something similar should happen to him again, John wrote himself some stern advice in his diary: "Let no trifling diversion or amusement or company decoy you from your books, i.e., let no girl, no gun, no cards, no flutes, no violins, no dress, no tobacco, no laziness decoy you from your books."

Though John knew that it would take some time to develop a list of clients in his new law practice, things were going slower than he had hoped.

Of course the situation gave him plenty of spare time to discuss politics with his friends.

As summer 1759 turned to fall, the seven-year French and Indian War finally drew to a close. British troops occupied Fort Ticonderoga and captured Quebec, bringing the seventy-five-year struggle for territory between Britain and France to an end. The French withdrew all their troops from North America, and the citizens of Braintree celebrated the great occasion with a day of prayer and fasting.

Most people were confident that a time of peace and prosperity would follow the end of the war. John, though, was not so sure, especially when in 1760 news reached Boston that King George II of Great Britain had died and his twenty-two-year-old grandson had ascended to the throne as King George III. This young King George had to face some grim facts. The French and Indian War had cost England millions of pounds. Added to this was the ongoing cost of keeping the French Canadians and the Indians they had conquered in line. The new king felt that the American colonists should help foot much of the bill for this, and to do this, he targeted trading practices in the colonies. American merchants traded with England, but they also traded directly with the French West Indies, Spain, and the Dutch islands in the Caribbean. The king decided that from now on all American merchants would have to pay heavy taxes on all products they imported or exported from the colonies.

Naturally enough the American merchants thought this approach was very unfair, and they set about finding ways to get around the new law. They unloaded their cargoes secretly in the dead of night or disguised what they were selling or bribed the American customs officials who were meant to be collecting the money for "mother" England.

When Parliament in England got word of how the colonists were flaunting the new law, they dusted off an old but seldom used law, giving customs officials the right to enter and search for smuggled goods in any colonist's home, office, warehouse, or ship. This new law was called a writ of assistance because it was made to assist customs officers in collecting taxes.

Boston's merchants were shocked by this turn of events. They knew they were British subjects, but why, they argued, did that give Parliament the right to send someone into their homes at any time of day or night? After all, there were no colonial representatives in the British parliament to represent or stand up for the rights of the American colonists. The merchants quickly banded together to challenge writs of assistance in court.

In February 1761 the case was heard before the superior court in Boston. Early in the morning on the day of the trial, John gathered up his quill, ink pot, and a notebook and set off for the court. He had to push his way past the merchants and other important citizens of Boston who also wanted to observe the proceeding. John finally found a seat at a table and spread out his notebook, ready to take notes on the important arguments of the case. Two of the men who helped him get accepted to the bar in Boston were to argue the case: Jeremiah Gridley would argue the king's side, while James Otis would argue against writs of assistance being issued in the colonies.

A long wooden table ran across the front of the courtroom. John watched as Chief Justice Hutchinson and four other judges took their places behind it. Each judge wore a crimson robe and an enormous white curly wig. The noise in the room quickly died down as the judges entered. Everyone waited eagerly for the lawyers' arguments to begin.

With a crack of the gavel, Chief Justice Hutchinson called the court to order, and Jeremiah Gridley rose to present his case. "There is no doubt that history supports the right of the king and Parliament to make laws for the colonies," he began.

John scribbled down in his notebook the gist of what was being said as Jeremiah clearly and logically laid out his argument to justify the use of writs of assistance in the colonies.

When the king's attorney was done, he sat down, and James Otis rose to his feet. James had always been a dynamic speaker, and he held nothing back as he presented his argument. His face was flushed, and the gaze of his steely eyes seemed to go from individual to individual in the packed courtroom.

"A man's house is his castle," James thundered. "And while he is quiet, he is as well guarded as a prince in his castle. This writ, if it should be declared legal, would totally annihilate this privilege." James went on speaking for three hours, laying out in minute detail the source of his disagreement with the king and Parliament on the legality of writs of assistance in the American colonies.

James was so passionate and so persuasive in the delivery of his argument that John soon stopped taking notes and laid down his quill. He marveled at the energy and the eloquence of the man. James was like fire unleashed in the courtroom.

At the end of the day, Chief Justice Hutchinson and the other four justices of the superior court did not rule on the case, choosing instead to wait for further input and instruction from England before they rendered their decision.

At home that night, John jotted down some notes to summarize the core of James Otis's argument. As he ended, John noted that every person who crowded in to view the case went away "as I did, ready to take up arms against writs of assistance.... Then and there the child Independence was born."

Three months after the court case, a particularly virulent strain of influenza spread through Massachusetts. It hit the elderly the hardest, and John began to be concerned when both his mother and his father came down with the illness. His mother survived, but his father did not. He died on May 25, 1761, at the age of seventy. Sixteen other elderly citizens of Braintree also died during the influenza outbreak.

The funeral for Deacon Adams, as most people knew him, was held on a warm spring morning. John and his brothers, Peter and Elihu, led the procession. Their mother was still ill in bed and was unable to attend the ceremony.

When the funeral was over, the will was opened and read. Things were pretty much as John had expected them to be. He inherited the second house on his father's property that had been rented out most of the time. He also received forty acres of land, which varied from pasture to woodland, swamp, and orchards. This was the smallest parcel of land his father bequeathed, as planned. John had received an expensive education and his two brothers had not, so they received bigger parcels of land. Peter inherited the rest of the land at Braintree, and Elihu received the farm their father had bought not long before in the neighboring village of Randolph. Their mother inherited the family home on the farm in Braintree, to live in until she died or remarried, at which time it would go to Peter.

When the reading of the will was over, John sat in the chair that had belonged to his father and looked around the room. There were so many reminders of him—the pipe on the mantelpiece, the gun hanging beside the door, and the felt hat he wore to church, a hand-me-down from his own father. As he viewed these items, John felt an overwhelming urge to write down some thoughts about his father. He found a quill and ink pot and turned the copy of the will over. On the back of it he wrote:

> The testor [John's father] had a good education, though not at college, and was a very capable and useful man. In his early life he

> was an officer in the militia, afterwards a deacon in the church, and a selectman of the town; almost all of the business of the town being managed by him in that department for twenty years together.

John laid his quill down and thought some more, then continued writing:

> A man of strict piety, and great integrity; much esteemed and beloved wherever he was known, which was not far, his sphere of life being not extensive.

That says it all, John thought as he wiped the quill clean. *Father never did travel far, but everyone who knew him respected and trusted him.*

The days after the funeral went on much as those before, but John felt lonely without his father to talk to. He often found himself thinking of a question to ask him about matters in Braintree, only to realize that his father was dead. To try to bury the loneliness he felt, John turned to hard work. He set out on a plan to improve his newly inherited property. He pulled up stumps, built stone walls, and planted a huge crop of corn and potatoes. He made improvements to the house as well. He had a lean-to kitchen built at the back, and he turned the original kitchen into a large, sunny office for himself.

One of John's friends was a thirty-five-year-old English clockmaker named Richard Cranch. In an attempt to take John's mind off the loss of his father, Richard invited John to accompany him on a visit to the Smith family at Weymouth. The Reverend William Smith and his wife, Elizabeth, had a son, William, and three daughters, Mary, Abigail, and Elizabeth. Richard was courting the oldest and prettiest of the three daughters.

John had seen the Smith girls at Colonel Quincy's home several times. Their mother belonged to the Quincy clan and was a cousin of the colonel's. He had never paid much attention to them because they were so much younger than he was. However, as he and Richard trotted their horses southward down the winding four-mile track from Braintree to Weymouth, John found himself interested in hearing about seventeen-year-old Abigail.

Richard told John that although she had never been to school, Abigail was one of the best-read young women he had ever met and that she had a lively interest in politics. *A young woman interested in politics? How uncommon,* John thought, and he looked forward to meeting her.

It was a half-hour ride from Braintree, and when they arrived in the seaside town of Weymouth, Richard turned his horse toward a large, two-story, L-shaped house. With its high wooden fence and immaculately laid-out front garden, it was much fancier than John's house.

As Richard and John were met at the door by one of the four slaves who served in the Smiths' home, John could hear laughter coming from somewhere inside the house.

Soon John was being introduced to Abigail Smith. Abigail had changed a great deal since the last time he had seen her. Though she was still short, at just under five feet tall, her black hair was now tied back, and her deep brown eyes locked onto his. *Here is a woman who is not afraid to look a man in the eye,* John thought as they were introduced, though not sure whether he liked her gaze or not.

He was not sure whether he liked some of Abigail's views on women, either. Although it took her a while to warm to the conversation, as the evening progressed, Abigail explained what she thought of the marriage laws. She had just finished a book by British writer Samuel Richardson, who had dared to write about the role of women in marriage and their right to an education. In eighteenth-century England and America, such ideas seemed strange. Once a woman married, it was assumed she would happily give up the right to own property or initiate any legal proceeding on her own. Her husband was there to protect her and to take the "burden" of such things away from her. But the radical new view of women's rights that Samuel Richardson had written about had fired Abigail's imagination.

"What do you think of Samuel Richardson's notion that a woman should only marry a man who is as intelligent as she is and who is willing to allow her to explore her own interests and ideas?" Abigail asked John.

For once John was stuck for words. He had never thought about marriage from a woman's perspective before. But he could not be blamed for that. Few men he knew, if any, thought of things from a woman's perspective.

The visit to the Smith home proved to be as stimulating as Richard had promised it would be. And by the time he left, John knew one thing for sure—Abigail Smith was a feisty, intelligent, and opinionated young woman. The trouble was, he just wasn't sure whether he liked her or not.

Yet over the following weeks, something kept drawing John back to the Smith house. First it was to borrow books that Parson Smith had generously offered to loan John. Abigail's father was also a graduate of Harvard, and the two of them enjoyed discussing the theological issues of the day. However, John soon began visiting whether he needed to borrow another book or not, and he found himself talking with Abigail more than with Parson Smith.

When John's work kept him from visiting Weymouth, he and Abigail wrote letters to each other. They were formal at first, but then they began to venture into teasing. Abigail wrote to John that she wanted to know what he really thought of her. He replied that among other things, she was a hopeless card player, had never learned to sing, and sat with her legs crossed. Abigail wrote back quickly, chiding John because "a gentleman has no business to concern himself about the legs of a lady!"

A year later, in November 1762, Richard Cranch and Abigail's older sister, Mary, were married. The wedding was large, and as it progressed, John found himself hoping that one day he would find himself in Richard's place, pledging marriage vows in front of Parson Smith to one of his daughters.

Chapter 6

The Stamp Act

It was a clear spring morning in 1764 when John rode up to his house. His mother came out from her house next door and hurried to meet him at the front door. "There's bad news," she said, wiping her hands on her apron. "There's smallpox in Boston!"

"Smallpox in Boston!" John exclaimed. "How many cases are there?"

Mrs. Adams shook her head. "I haven't heard any exact numbers, but Mrs. Smedley tells me half the town is down with it. I've been troubled about it all day. I think you and Peter must go and have the inoculation. It's too much of a risk for you to wait to catch it, and it would only be a matter of time, what with you going into Boston for your business."

John gulped. His mother was probably right. Smallpox was a terrible disease that swept through towns, leaving many people dead in its wake. And those who did not die were often left heavily scarred with pockmarks or blind. Once the disease took hold, nothing could be done for the patient. But there was something that could be done before a person caught the disease, though it was risky.

Fourteen years before John was born, back in 1721, his mother's uncle, Dr. Zabdiel Boylston of Brookline, had tried the first inoculation against smallpox in the American colonies. He did so at the urging of the Reverend Cotton Mather. The Reverend Mather had heard about the practice from his slave, who said he was inoculated against the disease as a child back in Africa. The inoculation involved taking a scab from a smallpox patient, mixing it with liquid, and puffing it up a healthy person's nose. Within a year of its first being tried in the colonies, many people were being inoculated. But inoculation killed about three percent of the people who tried it. However, this was a small risk when measured against the fifteen percent of people who died if they caught the disease naturally.

John was aware that the process of inoculation had changed some over the years. A piece of thread was now dipped into the puss from a smallpox sore, and then a slit was cut in the healthy person's arm. The infected thread was pulled through the wound with the hope that it would give the patient a light dose of the disease. Most times it worked that way; sometimes it did not. Still, John and his mother decided it was better for him to take the risk and get inoculated, since city folk were much more likely to contract smallpox and John was spending an increasing amount of time in Boston.

By now John and Abigail were engaged to be married, and Abigail had been hoping for a late spring wedding. But if John was going to be inoculated against smallpox, a late spring wedding would be impossible, as the inoculation was a time-consuming process.

John hated to break the news to Abigail, who immediately begged her mother to allow her to go to Boston with John so they could undergo the procedure together. But it was no use. Mrs. Smith did not believe in inoculations, and there was no way she was going to consent to her daughter's having one. So on Sunday, April 1, 1764, John and his brother Peter retreated to a room to prepare for the ordeal. For the next week they stayed there eating a diet of bread and milk, smoking an exotic plant that caused vomiting, and dosing up on mercury tablets.

When the seven days were up, the two Adams brothers rode slowly into Boston, where they met eight other men, including Samuel Quincy, Abigail's brother William, and her uncle, Cotton Tufts. They all checked into a temporary hospital set up at Castle William in Boston Harbor to have the inoculation.

Once the cut was made, the whole procedure took less than a minute. The men then had to stay in the hospital for three weeks, until any danger of their passing the disease on to someone else was over. Of course, like the others, John was anxious to see if he would get away with a light dose of the disease.

The men passed the days playing cards, reading, and talking. And they had a lot to talk about. There was the "proclamation line," which the British had set in October the year before and which was still a cause of annoyance to the colonists. In an attempt to keep the colonists and the Indians apart (so that the British would not need to spend so much on defending their borders), the king had issued a proclamation banning any settlements west of the Appalachian Mountains. Everything west of this proclamation line was reserved for the Indians forever. But the colonists were furious with the proclamation. Their population was expanding rapidly, and they believed they had the right to push westward with settlements into the fertile Ohio Valley.

There was a new problem for the men to discuss as well. News reached them during their isolation that Parliament in England had passed the Sugar Act. The Sugar Act cut in half the duty on molasses, which was used to make rum. This was seen as a good thing. The bad thing about the new act was that it decreed that all smuggling cases were now to be tried in admiralty court. In this court, judges, and not juries, rendered the verdict. This made a big difference in smuggling cases, since it was nearly impossible to get a colonial jury to convict a smuggler. What was even worse, the admiralty court was located in Nova Scotia. A person charged with smuggling had the added inconvenience of having to go there to have his case heard.

John was eager to get back to his legal books so that he could write an article for the newspaper pointing out how illegal this new act was. But he could not yet leave the hospital because of the risk of infecting others.

During his stay in the hospital, he greatly missed Abigail. The two had not been apart for this long since they had begun seeing each other. When he wrote to her, John was always careful to wash his hands first and wipe down the surface of the desk. But he still worried about inadvertently sending smallpox to her in the letters and advised Abigail to pass them through thick smoke to kill any trace of the disease before she opened them. He tried to be lighthearted in his letters, though in one he did confess:

> Don't conclude from any thing I have written that I think inoculation a light matter: a long and total abstinence for every thing in nature that has any taste, two heavy [medications that lead to] vomits, one heavy cathartic, four and twenty mercurial and antimonial pills, and three weeks close confinement to an house, are, according to my estimation of things, no small matters.

He did go on, however, to add that all the inconveniences were preferable to living in fear of the disease.

A week into his confinement, John became ill with chills and fever. Then a few smallpox sores broke out on his body, which he compared with his friends'. John had one of the lightest cases of the disease, and with the fear of dying behind him, he looked forward to seeing Abigail again and setting a wedding date.

When John and his friends finally got out of the hospital in May, they celebrated with a meal of oysters in a waterfront tavern. However, John's real celebration began when he finally got back to the parsonage at Weymouth. He and Abigail had been apart for forty days.

The happy couple set their wedding date for October 25, 1764, two weeks before Abigail's twentieth birthday. The two of them spent the summer preparing their home. Abigail also went to Boston to visit her aunt and uncle. While there she got sick with a stomach ailment, leaving John with the task of hiring household help and buying furniture. The furniture buying proved easy, but finding servants was much more difficult. Although Abigail's parents owned slaves, John could not bring himself to buy one of his own. Owning slaves did not sit well with his conscience. Eventually, when he had exhausted all the possibilities of hiring a servant, he accepted his mother's offer to loan him Judah, one of her free black servants.

As the wedding day approached, Abigail's health improved and she was able to take part in the final preparations. October 25 was a cool, clear day, and John rode to Weymouth early in the morning. At ten o'clock, with all the guests assembled in the parlor of the Weymouth parsonage, Abigail descended the stairs. John beamed when he saw her. She had never looked more beautiful to him than at that moment, wearing a red-and-white dress and with her dark hair in ringlets. Soon the couple were standing in front of Parson Smith saying their vows. John was nervous, but once the wedding ceremony was over, he relaxed and enjoyed the party. Late that afternoon John and Abigail rode their horses back over the track from Weymouth to John's home in Braintree, where they would live.

Married life suited John well. Abigail enjoyed working with her hands, and she sewed his clothes, churned butter, and smoked fish and meat for winter. While she did this, John worked his small farm and continued to build up his law practice. Now that he was married to a member of the Quincy clan, he had many rich new clients seeking his services.

On Sundays after church, John and Abigail loved to read the weekly newspapers that arrived from Boston and discuss the events that were taking place in Boston and across the Atlantic Ocean in England.

In the four years since King George III had ascended to the throne, the situation between the colonies and England had grown steadily more tense. And now, when John visited Boston, he heard more and more angry talk about England from the colonists.

In January 1765 John had to ride into Boston in a heavy snowstorm to attend a court session. He hated to leave Abigail, as she was now pregnant, but he knew his mother would keep an eye on her, and she had Judah to help with the work.

While in Boston John received the sad news that lawyer Oxenbridge Thacher, who had helped him get elected to the Boston bar, had contracted smallpox and died. But he also heard some good news. John's old mentor, Jeremiah Gridley, who had also had a hand in getting him elected to the bar, invited him to join a club called Solidality. This was a new, private club made up of the most distinguished lawyers in the city and formed to discuss legal history and theory. John jumped at the opportunity to join. Within weeks, though, the men in the club were discussing not legal history and theory but current events. On March 22, 1765, the British parliament passed the Stamp Act. The new act would become law in the American colonies on November 1 that same year. When news of the Stamp Act reached Boston three weeks after it was passed, it created an immediate uproar.

John was as outraged as everyone else when he heard the provisions of the new law. Under the Stamp Act, a tax was to be paid on every piece of paper used in the colonies for anything other than a book or a letter. This meant that every pamphlet, deed, diploma, bill, bond, ship's paper, newspaper—even playing cards—had to have a stamp pasted on it. The stamps cost up to ten pounds each, depending upon the document they were to be used on.

After reading an account in the newspaper of why the Stamp Act was passed, John was furious.

He was particularly incensed by the remarks of Charles Townshend, a member of the British parliament, who tried to sum up the government's reasoning for passing the new act. Townshend said, "And now will these Americans, children planted by our care, nourished by our indulgence until they are grown to a degree of strength and opulence, and protected by our arms, will they grudge to contribute their mite to relieve us from the heavy weight of the burden which we lie under?"

John watched as furor over the Stamp Act grew. Ships lowered their flags to half-mast, and church bells tolled. John's second cousin, forty-two-year-old Samuel Adams, who served in the Massachusetts colonial legislature, was one of the leading voices raised against the act. John admired his cousin's forthrightness but not his business practices. As tax collector in Boston, Samuel "misplaced" eight thousand pounds, which the city eventually gave up asking questions about. But for all this, Samuel, a fellow Harvard graduate, had a sharp tongue and a passion for politics.

Massachusetts was not the only place where resentment over the new British taxes was fermenting. In Virginia emotions were beginning to bubble over. John read every Virginia newspaper he could get his hands on for news of what the colony's elected House of Burgesses was doing about the problem. On May 31, 1765, the House of Burgesses, with Patrick Henry as its leader, passed the Virginia Resolves, which called for all the colonies to unite against the terrible injustice of the Stamp Act before it was followed with even more harsh measures. It was the first time the colonies thought of banding together against the British. John was astounded by the audacity of the Virginia Resolves, though he knew they were right.

Meanwhile Samuel took more direct action. He joined a new organization called the Sons of Liberty, and everyone waited to see what the Sons of Liberty would do about the Stamp Act.

By now John was spending a lot more time in Boston than he was in Braintree because he now had many prominent clients there. On a hot Sunday morning, July 14, 1765, John's brother Peter burst into the room where he was staying. John's heart skipped a beat. "What's wrong?" he asked. "Is something the matter with Abigail?"

"Not if you call having a tiny daughter wrong!" grinned his brother.

"But it's not time. It's not due for three more weeks!" John exclaimed.

"Time or not, she's here," Peter said. "She is very small, but everything seems to be going well. Abigail says to tell you she is tired but very happy."

John was extremely relieved to hear that Abigail had survived childbirth, as many young mothers did not. He hurried home to see his new daughter, officially named Abigail after her mother, though from the day she was born she was known to everyone as Nabby.

Exactly a month after Nabby was born, on August 14, the Sons of Liberty met under a huge elm tree in front of Boston Town Hall. The group was very angry at the way England was treating the colonies and wanted those in power to know it. Soon a large mob gathered and began shouting, "Liberty, property, and no stamps!" An effigy of Andrew Oliver, the tax stamp distributor for Massachusetts, and a large boot representing Lord Bute, a minister in Parliament who had been key in getting the Stamp Act passed, were hung from the elm tree. But the mob was hungry for more action and marched to Andrew Oliver's house, where they used axes to break down the door. Oliver and his family barely escaped before the mob surged in and smashed everything in sight. The following day Oliver resigned from his position as tax stamp distributor. Eleven days later it was Lieutenant Governor Hutchinson's turn to have his home ransacked. When the mob had finished with the house, nothing was left but its stripped-bare frame.

John was horrified when he heard what had happened. He believed that Americans had rights, rights they needed to fight for, but with words, not violence. He fired back with an article titled "A Dissertation on the Canon and the Feudal Law" that was published in the *Boston Gazette.* Despite its complicated title, the article carried a simple message. John argued that Americans did not need to fight for their freedom from England; they needed to fight for the rights already available to them under British law. He wrote, "The true source of our suffering has been our timidity. We have been afraid to think.... Let us dare to read, think, speak, and write.... Let it be known that British liberties are not the grants of princes or parliaments."

Although John hoped that people would think carefully about his ideas, he had his doubts. The colonists were becoming increasingly ugly in their calls for reform from England. He followed up the article with a letter to the newspaper suggesting the idea of "mixed government." By this he meant that the American colonies should be governed by three branches of government. The legislative branch would make the laws, the executive branch would administer them, and the judicial branch would watch over the laws to make sure they did not infringe upon people's rights. This was a radical idea, but John believed it was necessary to keep the three main functions of government separate. No single person should be able to gather too much power, because no matter how good a person's intentions were, John was sure, giving any man too much power would tempt him to be dishonest and self-serving.

In October 1765 the leaders of the thirteen colonies were invited to New York City for a meeting regarding what to do about the Stamp Act that was soon to go into effect. Eight colonies accepted the daring invitation, and the event became known as the Stamp Act Congress. The leaders of the colonies who attended this meeting agreed that Parliament in England lacked the authority to levy taxes outside Great Britain. But what was more important about the meeting was the fact that the colonies were looking to each other to present a united colonial opposition to the Stamp Act.

As November 1, the day the Stamp Act was to go into effect, rolled around, gloom settled over the city of Boston and the surrounding areas. It was a gloom John felt personally. No one in Boston would use the tax stamps. This meant that no cargoes were being loaded or unloaded from ships, little business was conducted, and the courts were suspended. With no legal work for John to do, he returned to Braintree to wait out the situation. No one knew what would happen. For the time being, the rebellion in the colonies affected the colonists most, but eventually England would feel the effects of so much lost trade. What would the king and Parliament do then? Would the American colonies be in for more punishment? Such questions lingered as the first snow of winter blanketed Massachusetts.

Chapter 7

Staring at Each Other

John looked up from his book. Was that a horse whinnying in his yard? He walked to the window and drew back the curtain. Sure enough, a man was tying his horse to the hitching post. As the man turned, John recognized him as Jeremiah Gridley's assistant. John stepped outside to greet him. "What brings you all this way on such a cold morning?" he inquired, gesturing for the assistant to come inside.

"I have a message for you from Mr. Gridley," the man replied.

"Sit down by the fire. My wife will make us a cup of tea, and you can deliver your message."

"Thank you, sir," the visitor replied. "There's been a town meeting in Boston, and the people there have elected three lawyers to appear before

Governor Bernard to request permission for us all to conduct legal business again."

"Probably a good idea," John agreed. "There are few people in Braintree or Boston who are not feeling the effects of the tax stamp boycott. Is that the message Mr. Gridley sent you here to deliver?"

"Not all of it, sir," the assistant said. "He sent me to fetch you. Mr. Gridley, Mr. Otis, and you were the three men chosen to go before the governor."

John stared into the fire for a long moment. He could hardly believe it. *Yes,* he thought, *Jeremiah Gridley and James Otis were obvious choices; they are well-established lawyers. But I, John Adams, lawyer from Braintree, their third choice!* It seemed extraordinary to John that they would pick him. Yet the young man sitting by the fire was proof enough that they had.

An hour later John had kissed Abigail and Nabby good-bye and was riding to Boston with the messenger. As their horses ambled along, John thought of the things he would like to say to the governor. He decided to argue that people cannot be required to obey a law that is impossible to carry out. And since there were no tax stamps or tax stamp distributors to be found in Boston, it was impossible to buy and use tax stamps. John also wanted to point out that keeping the courts closed would only create more chaos.

When he arrived in Boston, John went straight to Jeremiah Gridley's office to begin work on the presentation. James Otis joined them later in the day, and John was shocked when James began to rant on about matters that had nothing to do with the Stamp Act. He listened carefully to everything James said and came to the sad conclusion that the man was starting to lose his grip on reality. Nevertheless James did make some good suggestions as to how the three men should make their case on behalf of the people of Boston.

The next day John and the two older lawyers donned their scarlet robes and powdered wigs and went before Governor Bernard. It was December 21, 1765. The governor listened carefully to what they said, even taking notes as they spoke. In the end, however, he said that he could not defy the king of England and allow the courts to reopen without using tax stamps on every piece of official paper. Despite this, some of the lower courts did reopen, though the superior court remained closed.

John returned to Braintree, since he could do no legal work without tax stamps. By Christmastime the situation had become difficult for many colonial families. Although John constantly fretted about where the money would come from, the truth was that his family could survive quite well on the vegetables and livestock from the farm. Thankfully, Abigail was a competent home manager, and she had stored away potatoes, corn, and cabbages, as well as many smoked hams, legs of mutton, and fish.

Despite the difficulties and concerns, John was invigorated by the response of the colonists to the Stamp Act. Looking back over the year, he wrote in his journal:

> The year 1765 has been the most remarkable year of my life.... In every colony, from Georgia to New-Hampshire inclusively, the stamp distributors and inspectors have been compelled, by the unconquerable rage of the people, to renounce their offices.... The people, even to the lowest ranks, have become more attentive to their liberties, more inquisitive about them, and more determined to defend them than they were ever before.

On Christmas Day, 1765, John and Abigail took Nabby to visit Abigail's Quincy grandparents, who lived not far away at Mount Wollaston. That night, after Nabby had fallen asleep, the couple sat beside the fire. John noticed that Abigail looked particularly glum, and he knew why without asking. She was lonely. Her sister Mary and Mary's husband, Richard, had recently moved north to Salem, Massachusetts. Mary's daughter, Betsy, was the same age as Nabby, and Abigail longed to see the two cousins together. Also, John's mother, whom Abigail had grown quite attached to, had recently married John Hall, an older man who lived in Braintree, and she had moved out of the neighboring house.

John, on the other hand, had many friends and more invitations to dinner in Boston than he could possibly accept. He realized that if things ever got back to "normal," he and Abigail would have to think seriously about moving into Boston so that they could spend more time together as a family.

On January 1, 1766, John turned to a fresh page in his journal and wrote down his thoughts:

> Severe cold, and a prospect of snow. We are now upon the beginning of a year of greater expectation than any that has passed before it. This year brings ruin or salvation to the British colonies. The eyes of all America are fixed on the British Parliament. In short, Britain and America are staring at each other; and they will probably stare more and more for some time.... It is said at New York, that private letters inform [Americans that] the great men [in London] are exceedingly irritated at the tumults in America, and are determined to enforce the [Stamp Act]. This irritable race, however, will have [to have] good luck to enforce it. They will find it a more obstinate war than the conquest of Canada and Louisiana.

As the New Year began, however, John's family had a battle much closer to home to fight—whooping cough, an often deadly infection. Much to John's dismay, both Abigail and seven-month-old Nabby came down with it. Abigail's mother came to nurse the sick pair, but it was many weeks before Abigail was well enough to get out of bed, and Nabby's illness lingered.

In the world outside the Adams home, things proceeded much as John had predicted they would.

Britain and America stared at each other, each waiting for the other to give in first.

In March John was elected as a Braintree selectman, as his father had been before him. The selectmen oversaw the public schools, road construction and maintenance, and other "services of many sorts." It was a voluntary position, but John welcomed the opportunity to become more involved in the affairs of the small town.

On May 16 John was in Boston visiting Jeremiah Gridley. Suddenly the streets were alive with people dancing and shouting. John rushed out to see what all the commotion was about. Someone thrust a special edition of the *Boston Gazette* into his hand. John's heart raced as he read:

> Glorious News, Boston, Friday 11 o'clock, 16 May 1766. This instant arrived here the Brig Harrison, belonging to John Hancock, Esq; Captain Shubael Coffin, in 6 Weeks and 2 Days from LONDON, with important News, as follows.
>
> From the London Gazette.
>
> Westminster, March 18, 1766
>
> An ACT of REPEAL an Act made in the last Session of Parliament, included, an Act for granting and applying certain Stamp-Duties and other Duties in the British Colonies and Plantations in America, towards further defraying the expenses of defending, protecting and securing the same...

John impatiently scanned the article to the bottom, where he read that the British parliament had repealed the Stamp Act! He laughed out loud. America had stared down the great power of England! John wandered up and down the cobblestone streets shaking hands with the many revelers celebrating the victory with their fellow colonists.

As soon as his business in Boston was finished, John rode back to Braintree with the newspaper tucked in his saddlebag. He couldn't wait to tell Abigail the great news.

Over the next few weeks, John found out the details of why the British parliament had repealed the act. It seemed that George Grenville had had a falling out with King George III and had been replaced as prime minister by Lord Rockingham (as Charles Watson-Wentworth was known). The refusal of the American colonists to trade with Great Britain was having a terrible economic effect on English merchants, who were clamoring for the Stamp Act to be repealed before they went bankrupt. The new prime minister had no option but to respond to the merchants' demands. If he did not, England's already weak economy would only become weaker. A bill repealing the Stamp Act was introduced into Parliament, and on March 17, 1766, King George III signed it into law.

Another act was passed by Parliament in London at the same time the Stamp Act was repealed. This new act concerned John a great deal, though hardly anyone else seemed to be bothered by it in the least. This new act was known as the Declaratory Act, which affirmed the right of the British parliament to "make laws and statutes of sufficient force and validity to bind the colonies and people of America...in all cases whatsoever." In other words, this time the colonies might have gotten away with forcing the repeal of an act of Parliament, but the hammer would come down hard on them if they ever tried to bully the British parliament again.

John tried to tell himself that it was only because he was a lawyer that he was concerned about the problems such a law could cause the colonists. Besides, he did not have much time to dwell on what England might do next. John was swamped with work. His growing renown as a lawyer now had him regularly going as far away as Concord, Cambridge, Worcester, and even the island of Martha's Vineyard to represent clients in court. He found himself absent from home for at least a week per month, often longer.

All this extra work meant that for the first time John did not have to be concerned about money. In fact, he had so much extra money that he started buying up small tracts of land around Braintree. His brother Peter had married and moved into his wife's house. John also bought the Adams family home next door to his own. This home came with a barn and fifty-three acres of land, some of which his father himself had broken in.

In August John decided to take Abigail to Salem to visit her sister Mary, Mary's husband Richard, and their baby, Betsy. Abigail reluctantly decided to leave Nabby with John's mother. The child still had a nasty cough, and Abigail did not want to risk her becoming sick again on the long, hot journey.

Neither John nor Abigail had been to Salem before, and the couple set out on their trip early in the morning. As they rolled along in their open carriage, John basked in the warm summer air. The sun shone brightly, making the various greens of the surrounding woods and farmland more vivid than usual. In Boston they stopped to have dinner with some friends and then traveled on to Medford, where they spent the night at an inn. The following morning they set out early again and arrived in Salem at lunchtime.

Abigail and Mary were delighted to see each other again. They had always been close and hated the fact that they now lived so far apart.

Over the next several days, John and Abigail, accompanied by Mary and Richard, took in the sights of Salem. They went to "witch's hill," where the victims of the Salem witch trials had been executed, admired the large, stately homes of rich merchants, and ambled through the narrow streets of Marblehead, the fishing village adjacent to Salem. But all too soon it was time for the Adamses to return home to Braintree.

As John traveled back from Salem, he thought about his future. Now that the Stamp Act fiasco was far behind and the political situation had settled down, he looked forward to a long and prosperous career as one of Boston's leading lawyers. He made a mental note to himself to write to a bookseller in London and put in a standing order for every new law book or pamphlet that was published.

Although John was right about becoming one of Boston's leading lawyers, the future was far from settled. Little did John know that in a year's time he would be fuming over the British parliament's newest demands on the colonies and fearing that America would soon be forced into more conflict with the motherland.

Chapter 8

Save Your Money and Save Your Country

Throughout the rest of the summer John continued to travel widely to conduct his law business and to attend court in Boston. He was busy and happy, especially when Abigail told him she was expecting another child, due in July the following year. All went well with the pregnancy, and by now little Nabby had regained her full health.

On July 11, 1767, John became the proud father of a son. They named him John Quincy after Abigail's grandfather, who, sadly, died suddenly two days later, on the day of the baby's christening.

After the christening the men in the family retired to the parlor of the Weymouth parsonage to smoke and discuss the only public topic of the day. Word had reached Boston that Lord Townshend, chancellor of the exchequer, and the British parliament had enacted a new set of laws, contained in what was known as the Townshend Revenue Act. This act established not an internal tax on goods, as the Stamp Act had done, but an external tax on paper, glass, lead, and tea imported into the American colonies from England.

Lord Townshend was apparently confident that the colonists would understand the difference between an internal tax and an external tax and accept the external tax as necessary. He could not have been more wrong. No one in the colonies cared whether the taxes they were being asked to pay came from selling colonial goods in England or from goods being imported into America. The bottom line was that the colonists were going to have to pay more taxes, and they did not like the idea at all.

Another provision of the Townshend Act also sounded a warning bell to John and many others. It called for the money gathered from fining people who violated the new act to be put into a special fund, which would be used to pay the salaries of the governors of the various colonies. Until this time the governors had all been paid from local taxes. In effect, this change meant that the British and not the local people would now be employing the governors. John was concerned that over time the governors would follow the wishes of their new employers and not keep the best interests of the colonists at heart.

The American colonists reacted immediately to the new act. The British might send goods to their land and tax those goods, but that did not mean that anyone had to buy them. A wave of determined rebellion spread throughout Massachusetts and the other colonies. "Save your money and save your country" became the rallying cry of the day. Women everywhere refused to buy the British goods they loved so much. Bolts of silk, taffeta, and worsted wool lay on store shelves, while colonial women wove their own cloth. Canisters of India's finest teas went unsold; colonial women served each other coffee and local herb teas. Abigail joined in the boycott of British goods with great pride, even though it meant more work for her.

In the midst of all this unrest, John's friend and mentor Jeremiah Gridley died. His funeral, the largest John had ever been to, was held on September 15, 1767. As a result of Jeremiah's death, many more people wanted to engage John's legal services.

By now Abigail and John were tired of being apart, especially since Nabby and Johnny, as John Quincy was called, were growing so fast. They discussed their options and decided it would be best to rent out their Braintree house and farm and move into Boston. Abigail was very happy about this because, although she liked Braintree, her sister Mary and her family had just moved into Boston from Salem.

The Adams family made the move to Boston in April 1768. But even as they moved, John had a few misgivings. He was reluctant to expose the children to all the diseases that circulated about in a city of sixteen thousand people, all packed onto a small peninsula.

Still, John and Abigail found a house they liked and rented it. It was located on Brattle Square and was known locally as the "white house." The house was much bigger than the farmhouse in Braintree, and it was right in the center of Boston. The courts, government buildings, and Faneuil Hall, Boston's meeting place and main market, were all within two blocks. The only drawback was the constant noise, especially at night. Although the Adams family had a grandfather clock, a wedding gift from Abigail's parents, most of the other families in the town did not and instead relied upon the night watchman to remind them of the time. The night watchman walked throughout the neighborhood during the night yelling out the turning of the hour. On top of this, there were all sorts of other noises. Drunken sailors wandered up from the waterfront, and stray pigs foraged in the trash. John was a heavier sleeper than Abigail, and he adjusted to the noise faster than she did.

A month later, in May 1768, John wondered whether he had done the right thing in moving his family to Boston. It was not the threat of disease or the noise at night he was concerned about but the threat of riots and house burnings. That month John Hancock's sloop *Liberty* was seized by one of the zealous new customs agents sent out from London to enforce the Townshend Act. The vessel was carrying a cargo of smuggled madeira wine, and many of the residents of Boston took to the streets to make known their displeasure over the vessel's seizure.

John supposed there were two reasons why the British had gone after John Hancock. First, they wanted to make an example out of him, showing what would happen to anyone, no matter how rich, who dared to defy the new Townshend Act. Second, John Hancock was the biggest financial supporter of men like Samuel Adams and the Sons of Liberty. In fact, John Adams was reasonably sure that Sam Adams had no money whatsoever and that John Hancock was paying all his bills. If the British could make the charges against John Hancock stick, they could cripple him financially and cut off a lot of money going to the colonial rebels.

The seizing of the *Liberty* caused a huge riot on the waterfront. During the melee, customs agents were beaten and a great deal of crown property along the wharves was smashed and thrown into Boston Harbor. Governor Bernard responded by sending an urgent request to England, asking for four regiments of soldiers and a gunship to be sent to help keep the peace and keep money from the Townshend Act flowing in.

John had been out of town defending a client when the "Liberty Riots" occurred, but he quickly became involved in the situation. John Hancock hired him to defend him against the seizure of his sloop and the charges of smuggling. It was a high-profile case and one that led John Adams to much soul searching. "To what object are my views directed?" he wrote in his journal. "Am I grasping at money, or scheming for power?" He thought of his private collection of law books, which grew with every delivery from London, and added, "Fame, fortune, power, say some, are the ends intended by the library. The service of God, country, clients, fellow men, say others. Which of these lies nearest my heart?" These were questions John grappled with as he brought John Hancock's case to trial. Hancock was charged with smuggling, and the fine, if he were convicted, was set at nine thousand pounds!

The results of the trial were mixed. John did not bother to argue that John Hancock was innocent. Rather, he argued that the Townshend Act was illegal and therefore did not have to be followed. When the trial was over, John Hancock had lost the *Liberty* and the vessel's cargo, but there was not enough evidence to convict him of smuggling, and he went free.

Despite the high-profile Hancock case, it was a dreary time for John, not made any easier by the birth of their third child on December 28, 1768. They named her Susanna after John's mother. She was a sickly little thing, and Abigail was beside herself with worry that the child might not live. John employed the best physician in Boston, Dr. Joseph Warren, to visit the house and offer advice to Abigail. Somehow, between them they managed to coax Susanna's feeble little body along.

Then, just after Christmas, John watched as little Johnny stood on a chair and peered out of the upper-story window. John was reveling in his son's curiosity when suddenly Johnny called, "Papa. Papa. Red men!"

John walked over to see what his son meant by this. As he looked down into the street below, his blood chilled. Marching toward them was a battalion of "red men," British soldiers dressed in their bright scarlet uniforms. John scooped up Johnny and dressed him warmly. "Come on," he said. "We'll tell your mama we are going out. There is history in the making today."

Five minutes later John was strolling down King Street to the Long Wharf with young Johnny riding on his shoulders. The smell of pungent coffee and spices from the West Indies filled the air, but John hardly noticed. His attention was fixed on the harbor, where a large British man-of-war, the name *Romney* boldly painted on her side, lay at anchor. John counted the ship's guns: twenty-five per side. The vessel was unloading redcoats into lighter boats that the men then rowed to the wharf.

Soon other Bostonians began to arrive and line the Long Wharf. They booed and jeered as each British soldier climbed up the ladder and onto the wooden pier. John watched quietly. He caught a glimpse of his cousin Samuel, who was yelling insults at the redcoats as they formed lines and began marching toward the common.

"It's a bad day for the colonies," John muttered to himself. "No amount of soldiers will be able to keep peace in the colonies unless Parliament makes laws that protect us all from being used."

"Look at that bird!" Johnny exclaimed, breaking John's concentration. John looked up to see a seagull with a fish in its mouth.

John and his son stayed until all the troops had landed from the *Romney*, and then they set out for home.

Abigail was waiting anxiously at the door for John. "What did you see?" she asked.

John pulled off his boots and sat down and described the scene to her.

"It doesn't sound good," she said. "How long will it take England to come to its senses?"

As time went by, the worst fears of John and Abigail were realized. Three more British regiments arrived in Boston, and they created a great deal of resentment among the local people. They camped on Boston Common and drilled in Brattle Square, right outside the Adamses' dining room windows. Although little Johnny loved the constant entertainment of marching and music, no one else in the house appreciated the disruption.

Life as a British soldier was harsh, and guards had to be placed in the streets at night to stop the men from deserting. These military guards challenged every man who came by them, demanding to know who they were and where they were going. This did not sit well with the independent-minded Bostonians, nor did the fact that as time went on many of the soldiers supplemented their meager wages with part-time civilian jobs. Samuel Adams had no trouble stirring up colonial workingmen who had been put out of their jobs by

British soldiers who were prepared to work for less money.

Everyone felt the effects of having so many British troops in town, and frequent shouting matches were heard between the troops and the local people.

Despite the commotion associated with having so many British troops stationed in town, John was busier than ever. He was even busier after James Otis was found smashing the windows of the statehouse and had to be tied up and taken into the country for a long "rest." His clients turned to John to take over their legal cases.

In February 1770 the Adams family found themselves in the midst of their own family drama. One-year-old Susanna was not doing well. She had never been healthy, but now Dr. Warren prepared John and Abigail for the worst news possible. He felt sure their young daughter was going to die. And he was right. During the night on February 4, Susanna Adams died and was buried two days later. John and Abigail were heartbroken. Neither of them seemed able to discuss the death; it was too painful for them to do so. The situation was not made any easier by the knowledge that Abigail was expecting another baby. She could barely stand the thought of it after battling so long to save Susanna.

As John and Abigail tried to grapple with their loss, political events around Boston continued to pull John toward the "patriot cause," as the colonial position had become known.

It was on April 22, 1769, a year after they had moved to Boston, that John had his next real opportunity to challenge the British in court. Like the Hancock case, this new case involved a ship—a brig called the *Pitt Packet.* This vessel was stopped and boarded by a British frigate off Marblehead, Massachusetts. The *Pitt Packet* was carrying a cargo of salt and was manned by an Irish crew. As the British sailors stormed aboard, several members of the ship's crew feared they were going to be taken prisoner and pressed into service in the Royal Navy, a common practice. Four sailors were cut off from the rest of the crew at the bow of the *Pitt Packet.* One of them, Michael Corbet, reached down, drew a line in the salt spread across the deck, and said to the British lieutenant leading the raid, "If you cross this line, I will consider it proof your intention is to press me into service in the navy. And if you cross it, then by the God of heaven, you are a dead man."

The British lieutenant smiled broadly and stepped across the line and tried to grab Michael Corbet. His hands trembling, Corbet grabbed a harpoon and drove it through the lieutenant's neck, killing him. Corbet and the three other sailors on the bow of the *Pitt Packet* were arrested and brought to Boston to stand trial in admiralty court for murder.

John defended the four sailors. At first John argued that the sailors should be tried before a jury rather than a judge in admiralty court, but this argument was rebuffed. So he tried a different tack. He argued that the killing of the British lieutenant had been justifiable homicide. To back up his case, John lugged a large leather-bound book of British law into court and cited the section that prohibited the impressment of sailors in America into service in the Royal Navy. Since the four sailors from the *Pitt Packet* had feared they were about to be pressed into service in the navy, and since the lieutenant had done nothing to allay their fear, John contended the killing of the lieutenant was justifiable. The judge in the case was swayed by this argument, and Michael Corbet and his three comrades were found not guilty. Once again John had beaten the British in court.

Once the *Pitt Packet* trial was over, John had hoped things would quiet down. However, he did not get his wish. Instead Boston was about to be pitched into the most violent incident of all. And John would find himself squarely in the middle of it.

Chapter 9

Facts Are Stubborn Things...

It was February 22, 1770, and John was returning from a trip to Weymouth when he encountered the crowd of nearly two thousand. They were marching in a funeral procession, and John watched as they passed. A large number of boys led the procession in front of the simple wood coffin. Behind came the men and women, most walking but some riding in elegant carriages.

"Whose funeral is this?" John asked the man standing near his horse.

The man looked up at John incredulously. "How could a resident of Boston not know whose funeral this is."

"I have been out of town for several days and only just returned," John replied.

"I'll tell you, then. This is the funeral of young Christopher Snider," the man said. "He was murdered by Ebenezer Richardson, one of the Crown's representatives, no less. There's anger in the air over the killing of such a young one."

The murder of twelve-year-old Christopher, shot while he and a group of boys taunted Ebenezer Richardson at his home, did indeed serve to make the already angry mood of Boston even angrier toward the British and, in particular, the soldiers still encamped on Boston Common. The residents of the city began to taunt the soldiers more than ever. They would pelt them with rocks and snowballs and yell "lobsterbacks" at them.

The British redcoats were under strict orders to avoid reacting to such confrontations when they occurred, but there was a seething distrust and hatred between the soldiers and the residents of Boston. To make matters even more unbearable for the redcoats, people kept setting fire to their barracks buildings and property.

On March 5, eleven days after Christopher Snider's funeral, snow fell on Boston, blanketing the streets several inches deep. That evening John went to a friend's house, where a group of men met regularly to discuss the political situation in Boston and the colonies. A fire was crackling in the fireplace as the men talked. Suddenly the sound of a volley of gunfire filled the room. Startled by the sound, John jumped up and ran to the window. In the distance, on King Street, he could see a mob of people yelling and running in all directions. John quickly donned his overcoat and headed out into the snow, followed by the other men.

When he reached the custom house on King Street, John could scarcely believe his eyes. The white snow had turned to scarlet with blood. Three bodies lay dead on the ground, and eight more bodies lay wounded and bleeding. In front of the custom house stood a group of British soldiers, their rifles at the ready and their bayonets attached, while an angry crowd hurled abuse, rocks, and snowballs at them. The wounded were dragged away, but two hours later one of them died, followed two days later by another man. In all five people were killed.

It wasn't until later that first evening that John learned the details of what had happened. It seemed that tensions had been running high between a group of British soldiers and several men who wove rope nearby on the waterfront. Several fights had broken out between the two groups during the days before, and this night the rope weavers had gone looking for another fight with the redcoats. When they could not find one, they focused their attention on the lone British sentry standing guard outside the custom house on King Street. At the same time, church bells had begun tolling continuously to warn of fire. Upon hearing the bells, people had come out from their homes to see where the fire was. It proved to be a false alarm, but seeing the group of men in front of the custom house, they gathered round to see what was happening.

The lone sentry, fearing for his life, sent a messenger to the British barracks for reinforcements. Soon seven soldiers under the command of Captain Thomas Preston arrived on the scene. With their rifles loaded and bayonets attached, they took up position along with the sentry in front of the custom house.

The angry crowd booed and jeered the soldiers and pelted them with snowballs. In the midst of the noisy, tense situation, someone yelled "fire." The redcoats, thinking it was Captain Preston, began shooting their rifles into the crowd. Soon afterwards more soldiers arrived, and order was finally restored to the streets. Captain Preston and the eight soldiers who had taken part in the shooting were arrested for murder.

After he had learned all the details of what would, as a result of the agitation of his cousin Samuel, become known as the Boston Massacre, John returned home, where Abigail waited anxiously to hear about what had happened.

The following morning John went to his office as usual. He had just settled down to work when one of his assistants brought a man into the room. John recognized him. He was a loyalist (loyal to the British crown at all cost) merchant named James Forrest. John shook his hand and offered him a seat.

After a few formalities the merchant came to the point. "Mr. Adams, I am sure you know the events of last night as well as any man in this town. And I am also sure that as a lawyer you have asked yourself the question 'Who in this town is going to defend Captain Thomas Preston and the eight British soldiers who are in jail at this moment, charged with murder?'"

John nodded. "Of course, a lawyer's mind does run that way," he said. "Do you know if they have found a lawyer yet?"

"That is why I am here," James responded with tears in his eyes. "Even the loyalist lawyers won't touch the case. But someone has to put the law above his personal feelings and take on this case. I am desperately hoping you will be that person."

John gulped. He dared not trust himself to speak. Who in his right mind would defend British soldiers against a mob incited by the Sons of Liberty? What if things got out of hand and the mob came after him, or Abigail and the children? Boston was a small enough town that everyone knew where he lived.

Then another question popped into John's mind. If he did not defend the soldiers, who would? And what better excuse would Parliament in England have for making more laws in Boston than accusing it of being a place where British justice was not carried out?

Before he could change his mind, John spoke up. "All right, sir. I will take the case. How soon can you arrange for me to interview my clients?"

That night, as John walked the long way home, he rehearsed how he would tell Abigail what he had done. But when he explained the situation to her, she agreed to stand behind him one hundred percent, even if it cost them friends and business, or even more. That night before going to bed, John wrote in his diary: "She [Abigail] was very sensible of all the danger to her and to our children as well as to me, but she thought I had done as I ought, she was very willing to share in all that was to come and place her trust in providence."

John's first priority was to get the trial of the British soldiers delayed until October so that frayed tempers could cool. His next move was to have two separate trials—one for Captain Preston and one for the soldiers—as he planned to use different defenses for them.

Six weeks later a ship sailed into Boston Harbor bearing news that the British parliament had repealed all but one portion of the Townshend Act. Ironically, the repeal had occurred on the exact same day as the Boston Massacre had taken place. The only portion of the Townshend Act left in place was a tax on tea. The colonists did not concern themselves about this, since they had taken to smuggling in large amounts of the much cheaper Dutch tea.

On May 29, 1770, nearly three months after the Boston Massacre, Abigail delivered another son, whom she and John named Charles. Thankfully, Charles was a robust child from the start and not sickly like Susanna had been, which meant that the baby's health was one less thing for John to be concerned about.

A week after Charles's birth, the Boston town meeting elected John as a representative to the

Massachusetts legislature. When he told Abigail about it, she burst into tears. The appointment would mean that he would have even less time to spend with his growing family and less time to make money at his law practice. However, after a few minutes Abigail composed herself and assured John that she was willing to support him and his convictions about the political situation in the colony no matter what sacrifice that involved.

That night John could not sleep. He lay awake for hours thinking about what the future might hold for him. Being in politics was like walking a tightrope: One small slip in any direction and he could fall off. And what a fall it could be! The British were not above trying a colonial politician for treason if they thought he was undermining their rule in the colonies. John would have to be very careful in his dealings if he did not want to meet that fate.

Governor Hutchinson of Massachusetts had ordered the legislators to meet in Cambridge rather than in the Boston town house because he was worried about a mob attacking them. This added at least an hour of travel to John's day, as he had to take the ferry back and forth to Cambridge. When he was not in Cambridge, John continued to work on his defense of Captain Preston and the British soldiers.

The first trial, that of Captain Thomas Preston, was held in October. In the trial John was assisted by Josiah Quincy Jr., one of Abigail's cousins, and Josiah's brother Samuel. Robert Treat Paine was the prosecutor for the Crown.

The defense's argument was simple. Captain Preston had not fired a shot himself, nor had he ordered his men to do so. The men had shot into the crowd without an order so as to defend themselves against a mob they thought were out for their blood. Much to John's relief, Thomas Preston was found not guilty and quickly returned to England.

In the second trial, which was held in early December, John argued that the soldiers should not be blamed for the massacre but rather that the mob was responsible for it. And even then the mob was not fully to blame. The people had been incited to act by the governor's foolhardy policy of quartering English troops on Boston Common, where the soldiers' presence annoyed everyone in the city. John described the confusion the mob had caused and how in that confusion the soldiers believed they had heard their captain order them to fire. So as far as they were concerned, they were just following orders. What was more, the prosecution had witnesses to prove that only two of the soldiers actually fired their rifles.

John concluded his defense with this statement: "Facts are stubborn things, and whatever may be our wishes, our inclinations, or the dictums of our passions, they cannot alter the state of facts and evidence."

Two hours later the jury returned their verdict. They found six of the soldiers not guilty and found the other two guilty of manslaughter. Since it was their first offense, as punishment both soldiers were branded on their thumbs and discharged from the army.

John was very proud of the job he had done in defending Captain Preston and the British soldiers, but he had to be careful not to seem too pleased with himself. A lot of people in Boston were angry over the acquittals and had hoped to see a public hanging. Still, no one attacked John or his family.

John's work continued until the following spring, when the strain of all that had gone on made him ill. John's heart beat irregularly, and his chest and lungs burned with pain.

Dr. Warren was called, and he sat with John all night, fearing that he might not make it through till morning. While John did live to see daybreak, he was still a very sick man. Dr. Warren insisted that he needed complete bed rest for at least a month, and so the Adamses decided to move back to their house in Braintree. That way they would be close to John's mother and in the fresh country air once again.

John could not help with the move, and once again he was grateful that he had married such a capable woman who could take care of all the arrangements. He kept his law office in Boston. His two clerks would take care of the routine business until he was well enough to ride into town to tend to business himself.

In Braintree John was once again far from the political hotbed of Boston, and his interest in politics began to wane. As his strength returned, he looked forward to building up his law business once again. He even wrote “Farewell politics!” in his diary in large letters. But it was not going to be that simple.

Chapter 10

Intolerable Acts

The next sixteen months were pleasant ones for the Adams family. Everyone remained healthy, and on September 15, 1772, Abigail gave birth to another son, whom they named Thomas Boylston. He was a big, strong boy.

John had been keeping a steady eye on the situation in Boston, and by July he had come to the conclusion that the worst of the rabble-rousing was over and the situation with Britain was stable. He decided to buy a house in Boston and move the family back there. Furthermore, he promised himself in his journal that he would not get involved with his cousin Samuel's attempts to stir up the public. He wrote, "Above all things, I must avoid politics, political clubs, town meetings, general court, etc. etc. etc." Instead he decided that at thirty-six years of age all the "fight" was behind him. "What an atom, an animalcule I am—the remainder of my days I shall rather decline, in sense, spirit, and activity. My season for acquiring knowledge is past. And yet I have my own and my children's fortunes to make. My boyish habits, and airs are not yet worn off."

Although John lamented that he had "yet to make his fortune," he was, in fact, doing better than most of his peers. He and Abigail bought a large brick house on Queen Street for 533 pounds, as much as a skilled craftsman would earn in four years.

John's resolve to stay out of politics did not last more than a few months. Politics drew him like a magnet. Toward the end of 1772, Samuel Adams convinced him to stand for a seat in the governor's council. John won the election but never got to take the position because Governor Hutchinson refused to give him a seat, believing his views were too radical.

Several months later, in March 1773, another situation attracted John's attention. This time not only were the British going to take over paying the governor's salary but they were also going to start paying all the judges. This meant, of course, that the judges would be employed not by the people of Boston but by the king of England.

Samuel Adams used the situation to stir up trouble in Boston. But he did not have to try hard; everyone could see that the judges would soon be making decisions that would make their employer happy.

Matters were made worse when Benjamin Franklin, who was the London agent for the Massachusetts House of Representatives, got hold of some letters Governor Hutchinson had sent to an English politician. When the letters were published in the *Boston Gazette*, John was outraged. They exposed the governor as a man who wanted to curb the colonists' rights. One clause from one of the letters read, "there must be an abridgement of what are called English liberties [in the colonies]." Once again Samuel Adams had fuel to add to the fire of public discontent.

But neither of these events had anything like the electrifying effect on Boston that a change in the tea tax had. When the Townshend Act was repealed, the only tax left in place was that on tea. But now the British East India Company, which operated under a royal charter, found itself with more than eighteen million pounds of tea on its hands. To help the company out, Parliament had passed a new law reducing the tax on tea in the colonies from ninepence a pound to threepence and had given the East India Company the monopoly for importing teas into the colonies.

While this seemed a reasonable thing to do, it set off a powder keg of protest in Boston. The reduced taxes made English tea cheaper than the smuggled Dutch tea that most of the colonists had become used to drinking. But even though the tax was lower than before and the tea cheaper, the new law served to remind the colonists that they still had an unfair tax levied on their tea. Merchants were also concerned that if Parliament could so easily give a monopoly to the East India Company to import tea into the colonies, it could just as easily give monopolies to other companies for other commodities imported to America. Such action would put the merchants out of business.

Given all of this, Samuel Adams and the Sons of Liberty managed to convince the people of Boston that the ships bringing the new, bargain-priced tea to Massachusetts should be turned back to England.

When the *Dartmouth* tied up at Griffin's Wharf in Boston, the Sons of Liberty were there to make sure no tea was off-loaded. Days went by, and soon thousands of men from the countryside surged into Boston to protest and help turn the ship back. Two more ships, the *Eleanor* and the *Beaver,* tied up alongside the *Dartmouth,* but none of the ships were able to off-load their cargo of tea.

During this time John tried to keep out of trouble. He went about his law business and spent several weeks arguing a case at the Plymouth courthouse.

Around lunchtime on Friday, December 17, 1773, John rode back from Plymouth. When he reached the outskirts of Boston, he noticed many more people than usual milling around on the streets. He quickened his horse's pace, eager to get home to Abigail and learn what had been going on.

John burst into the house to be met by three-year-old Charles. "Papa," the boy said, his eyes shining, "the Indians came last night and put tea in the water!"

Just then Abigail came up behind Charles. She laughed. "Well, your son has the right idea. Let me tell you all the details."

It took Abigail only about ten minutes to explain what had happened the night before. Under cover of darkness, a sizable group of men and boys disguised as Indians had seized control of the three British ships carrying tea. These "Indians" had then dragged 340 chests of tea from the vessels' holds and dumped them overboard into Boston Harbor. This amounted to nine thousand pounds worth of tea.

John was thrilled when he heard this. "Why, Abigail," he said, "what a magnificent thing to do! The people should never rise without doing something to be remembered, something notable and striking. And they surely did that. The destruction of the tea was such a bold move that I am sure it will have long-reaching consequences."

"What do you think Parliament will do?" Abigail asked, lifting one-year-old Tommy onto her knee.

John shook his head. "It's very hard to say. They might well punish us by sending more troops or by adding more taxes and duties."

As the weeks passed after the Boston Tea Party, as the event quickly became known, John began to wonder whether the British were going to do anything in response. Then, in early February 1774, Massachusetts got word of England's response. It was shockingly harsh, and John could hardly believe it. Parliament had passed the Port Act, closing Boston Harbor. The custom house was to be transferred south to Plymouth, and the seat of provincial government to Salem. As if this were not devastating enough for the Massachusetts colony, Parliament also passed the Massachusetts Government Act, which made it illegal to have more than one town meeting a year and gave the king the right to appoint or remove all sheriffs and judges. In addition, more British troops would be sent to maintain order. All of these measures would stay in effect until the colony paid nine thousand pounds to cover the cost of the tea dumped into the harbor. The colonists soon dubbed these acts the Intolerable Acts because they placed what the people considered an intolerable and unbearable burden upon them.

Next, the *Massachusetts Spy* published King George III's speech at the opening of Parliament. The king's message could not have been plainer. "We are not entering into a dispute between internal and external taxes, nor between taxes laid for the purpose of revenues and taxes laid for the regulation of trade, nor between representation and taxation; *but we are now to dispute whether we have, or have not any authority in that country [America].*"

John was appalled by what the British had done to them. He was sure it meant the end of Boston. He was so sure, in fact, that he wrote, "The town of Boston, for ought I can see, must suffer martyrdom. It must expire. And our principal consolation is that it dies in a noble cause: the cause of truth, of virtue, of liberty, and of humanity."

Once again Boston was occupied by British troops: four regiments of infantry and three of artillery. The troops marched up and down the streets and goaded the hundreds of men who had been put out of work by the closing of the harbor.

In the midst of all this, something happened that neither John nor the British had foreseen. The other American colonies, having heard about the plight of the people of Boston, began to send food and money. Some food and money even came from a group of Englishmen who backed the colonies' rights to set their own taxes. The other colonies had realized that it was not just one colony under attack but all of them.

On June 17, 1774, the Massachusetts assembly met illegally and voted to send four delegates to a proposed meeting of representatives from all the colonies. The gathering was being called a Continental Congress. John Adams, Samuel Adams, James Bowdoin, and Robert Treat Paine would be Massachusetts' delegates. The date of September 6, six weeks away, was set for the representatives to meet at Carpenter's Hall in Philadelphia. John recorded in his journal on Monday, June 20, his thoughts about his nomination as a representative.

> This is a new and a grand scene open before me: a Congress. This will be an assembly of the wisest men upon the continent, who are Americans in principle: that is, against the taxation of Americans by the

> authority of Parliament. I feel myself unequal to this business. A more extensive knowledge of the realm, the colonies, and of commerce, as well as of law and policy, is necessary, than I am master of. What can be done? Will it be expedient to propose an annual congress of committees? to petition? Will it do to petition at all?—to the King? to the Lords? to the Commons? What will such consultations avail?

No sooner had John been nominated than he began to have doubts about going. He wondered whether he knew enough about English law to be of much use, and several friends tried to persuade him to give up the position, reminding him that it was very dangerous to defy a country as large and powerful as Great Britain.

The following Friday John once again poured out his feelings in his journal:

> The objects before me are too grand and multifarious for my comprehension. We have no men fit for the times. We are deficient of genius, in education, in travel, in fortune, in everything. I feel unutterable anxiety. God grant us wisdom and fortitude! Should the opposition be suppressed, should this country submit, what infamy and ruin! God forbid. Death in any form is less terrible!

There had never been a meeting like it before, and the longer John waited to go, the more nervous he became. He confided in a letter to a friend, "I am at a loss, totally at a loss, what to do when we get there; but I hope to be there taught. It is to be a school of political prophets, I suppose, a nursery of American statesmen."

In the meantime John had much to do before he left. He moved the family back to the relative safety of Braintree. And there was the harvest to prepare for, something Abigail would have to oversee while he was gone. Bringing in and storing the crops was more important now than ever, since the harbor was closed. With the political unrest, the local school had also been closed. John made out a series of studies in French, Greek, Latin, history, and philosophy for nine-year-old Nabby and seven-year-old Johnny to follow. And since there was not much work for his assistant, John Thaxter, to do, John asked him to tutor the children part-time under Abigail's watchful eye.

John was relieved when Mary and Richard Cranch and their growing brood of children also moved out of Boston and back to Braintree. At least Abigail would have some company while he was away in Philadelphia.

Eventually the time came for John to leave for the Continental Congress. He said good-bye to the children, and Abigail accompanied him to Boston, where he met up with the other three delegates going to the meeting. James Bowdoin, a wealthy merchant, had turned down the appointment because he had not had a smallpox inoculation and Philadelphia was well known for its deadly epidemics. Thomas Cushing had been selected to go in his place.

Once in Boston, John felt the weight of the responsibility that had been placed upon him. It seemed that everyone expected some kind of miracle to happen in Philadelphia.

Early on Wednesday morning, August 10, 1774, John Adams, Samuel Adams, Robert Treat Paine, and Thomas Cushing were officially bid farewell before setting out. On the journey they rode in Thomas Cushing's hansom and were accompanied by six servants. The weather was particularly hot, and the road was rutted and dusty. By Saturday they had reached Hartford, Connecticut, where they spent two days resting and meeting several of the Connecticut delegates, who were also about to set out for Philadelphia. Ten days after leaving Boston they arrived in New York City, where they spent several days resting and taking in the sights of the city. It was the first time John had ever been outside of New England, and he was very impressed by what he saw.

From New York the group made their way to Princeton, New Jersey, where again they spent several days resting. During the stay in Princeton, John took the opportunity to explore the university located there. From Princeton the men traveled on to Philadelphia, arriving on August 29, nineteen days after setting out from Boston.

Philadelphia was very different from Boston. Its population was nearly twice that of Boston's. Like Boston, it was a port city, and wharves stretched along the edge of the Delaware River for two miles, with ships of all shapes and sizes tied up alongside them. However, unlike Boston, which was a maze of tangled, narrow streets, Philadelphia had broad, tree-lined avenues that were laid out in a grid pattern. And the city had lots of parks and open spaces. Stately houses lined the streets, and the city's public buildings were large and impressive. John was captivated by all he saw in Philadelphia.

On September 5 fifty-five delegates from twelve colonies met at Carpenter's Hall. (The thirteenth colony, Georgia, did not send any delegates.) At first the men were rather quiet. Most of them, although well known in their own colonies, had never heard of each other. However, as they dined and talked together, they soon came to know each other's strengths and ideas.

It did not take John long to find out that about half the delegates were lawyers, many of whom were very rich men. One man John was particularly impressed with was Colonel George Washington, the six-foot-four-inch-tall delegate from Virginia. He did not talk as much as some of the other men present, but when he spoke, others listened. John wished he had that same command over his fellow delegates.

Privately John thought that England and Massachusetts would eventually be at war with each other, but he dared not voice this opinion to the other delegates. They did not have redcoats camped out on their commons or English men-of-war blocking their harbors. Apart from some bothersome import taxes, they felt at peace. Since John doubted they would feel any urgency to shed the blood of their citizens in Massachusetts, he concentrated on getting the rest of the delegates to support an embargo on British goods. It was about all he felt he could expect of them.

For a long time it seemed the men would not be able to agree on even that much. Other issues had to be resolved first. The delegates had to work out the fairest way to vote on issues. Some delegates argued that they should have a different number of votes for each colony depending upon how many people lived in that colony. This led to a debate on whether or not black slaves should be counted in that number. Other delegates, however, argued that the number of votes a colony had should be based upon that colony's wealth. The delegates even argued about the type of prayer that should be used at the convention. Most of the New England delegation was Congregationalist like John, while many of the Virginians were Episcopalians and a number of the Pennsylvania delegates were Quakers. John began to despair that they would get anything constructive accomplished during the Congress.

John expressed his frustration in a letter home. "The business of the Congress is tedious, beyond expression. This assembly is like no other that ever existed. Every man in it is a great man—an orator, a critic, a statesman, and therefore every man upon every question must show his oratory, his criticism, and his political abilities."

During his time in Philadelphia, John looked forward to receiving letters from home, though they did not come as frequently as he would have liked. The postal service was poor: A letter could take two weeks to get from Braintree to Philadelphia. In her letters Abigail wrote about many things—the good harvest, a broken plow, the price of fish, and her own fears that the colonies would end up going to war with the British. She described observing the British mount a cannon on Beacon Hill and another on the Boston Neck. In addition, a regiment of redcoats was now encamped on the Neck. Although John was chilled by this information, he was glad Abigail took the time to write about it to him. He often learned more about what the British were doing through her than he did from his official sources. Sometimes he even read quotes from her letters to the Congress.

Enclosed in one of Abigail's letters was a letter from Johnny. As John read it he smiled. He imagined his son huddled over his paper at the kitchen table, writing.

> Sir:
>
> I have been trying ever since you went away to learn to write you a Letter. I shall make poor work of it, but Sir Mamma says you will accept my endeavors, and that my Duty to you may be expressed in poor writing as well as good.

> I hope to grow a better Boy and that you will have no occasion to be ashamed of me when you return. Mr. Thaxter says I learn my Books well—he is a very good Master. I read my Books to Mamma. We all long to see you; I am Sir your Dutiful Son, John Quincy Adams.

John often tucked the letters from home in his jacket pocket and reread them when he had a spare moment, not that he had many of them. He was soon elected to the Rights and Grievances Committee, whose task it was to spell out the ways in which the rights of the colonists had been violated and what they expected England to do to correct such wrongs.

The Continental Congress ended on October 25, 1774, and by their final meeting, the delegates had reached several important decisions. First, all trade to and from England would be cut off in a year unless the Intolerable Acts were repealed by then. Second, the Congress issued a Declaration of Rights, which asserted that Americans were entitled to the same liberties as the citizens of England enjoyed. And third, the delegates would meet again the following May if England had not backed down.

On October 28 John started the arduous trip back home. As the carriage rumbled away from Philadelphia and into the countryside, John noticed many militia groups drilling. He wondered how Great Britain would respond to the list of grievances that he and Virginia delegate Patrick

Henry had drawn up. Would they back down from their demand on America, or was the country marching irrevocably toward war?

Chapter 11

Up in Smoke

Five months after arriving back in Braintree from the Continental Congress, John saw any hope of a peaceful resolution to the colonies' grievances with England go up in smoke—the smoke of guns fired in Lexington and Concord, Massachusetts.

Around midmorning on Wednesday, April 19, 1775, as John was going over the farm account books, a messenger galloped up to the door of the house.

"Draw water for the horse," John yelled to his oldest son as he flung the door open to see what the messenger wanted. Whatever it was must be urgent because his horse was breathless and frothing at the mouth. "What is it?" he asked quickly.

"General Gage set the British marching out of Boston in the night," the messenger replied, wiping his sweaty brow. "It was meant to be a secret, but who can keep a secret in Boston these days? There are too many men about with nothing to do but keep their ears open. Anyway, Dr. Warren got word that they were marching to Lexington to arrest Samuel Adams and John Hancock, who were staying with the minister there. From there they have orders to march on to Concord and seize the patriots' ammunition supply."

"Well, what happened?" John asked.

"Having got wind of the scheme, Dr. Warren sent off William Dawes and Paul Revere by two different routes to warn all the militia groups between Boston and Lexington. It was a tricky task, with all the British roadblocks out of Boston, but Paul Revere got through to Lexington first and roused Captain Parker and the militia. At four-thirty in the morning, six hundred British soldiers came marching into town. Seventy patriots were facing them. Someone gave the order to fire, and it was all over in a couple of minutes. Captain Parker and seven of his men were killed, ten more were wounded, and the British walked about like they owned the place."

"And what of Samuel Adams and John Hancock?" John inquired.

"Ah, they managed to flee long before the British arrived," the messenger replied.

"Would you come in for soup?"

John turned to see Abigail standing behind him. "Oh, yes, please do," he added to his wife's invitation. "In all of this excitement I have quite forgotten my manners. Abigail, did you hear—the British have marched!"

"No, no. I don't have time to eat. Thank you all the same, ma'am," the messenger replied. "There's really not much else to tell. We think the British are marching on to Concord right now, and I'm riding through the countryside calling militias to come to the aid of Concord." He turned to Johnny and ruffled the boy's hair. "Thank you for watering my horse. You've done a service for your country this morning."

Johnny grinned back at the messenger.

Twenty-four hours passed before the Adams family heard what happened next. The British did indeed march on to Concord, not knowing that the men there had worked all night to hide their ammunition supplies. When the 150 patriots defending Concord saw 600 British soldiers approaching, decked out in crimson uniforms with shiny brass buttons and marching in precise lines, they withdrew from the town across the Concord River at North Bridge and took up positions in the nearby hills.

The British spent the morning searching for the ammunition cache, but they had no luck finding it. Meanwhile, militia groups from nearby towns, shouldering their muskets, marched to the scene. The battle that followed was something the British had never before encountered. The colonists did not line up in columns and fight like "soldiers." Instead, small groups of them ambushed the redcoats, catching them totally off guard.

By nightfall the British were beating a disorganized retreat. General Gage sent out a British rescue party of one thousand soldiers to bring them safely back to Boston. But the whole operation soon became a nightmare for them. By then four thousand militiamen waited behind the trees and stone walls that lined the route back to Boston, picking off redcoats as they retreated. When the British soldiers finally did reenter Boston, they were short 273 men, either dead or missing. The patriot militiamen had lost only half that number in the fighting.

A few days later John learned that militiamen from the surrounding colonies had come to help Massachusetts. Together, ten thousand colonial troops surrounded Boston, containing the British to the city. There would be no more military forays into the New England countryside for the redcoats.

All of this stirred up two very different emotions within John. On the one hand, he was glad that something significant had finally happened. Now the delegates who had sat on the fence at the Continental Congress would understand just what the British were capable of when they were crossed. On the other hand, John felt a certain amount of dread. In a week he was supposed to be heading back to Philadelphia for the second Continental Congress. But now that "war" had broken out, he wondered how he could leave Abigail with four young children so close to the fighting.

John offered to stay home, but Abigail would not hear of it. She reminded him that his two brothers, Peter and Elihu, who were in the local militia, both lived nearby. And she pointed out that she would have plenty of other company. A steady stream of refugees from Boston either walked or rode past the Braintree farmhouse each day, and Abigail had already put up several passing militia regiments in the house and barn. She told John that everyone had to do his or her duty during such difficult times, and his duty was to go to the Continental Congress. However, when the other New England delegates, who now included John Hancock, set out for Philadelphia at the beginning of May, John Adams was not among them. A fever had kept him at home in bed.

Still, John was determined to start out for Philadelphia as soon as he possibly could. Two days later, when the fever started to abate, he borrowed his father-in-law's sulky and horse, hired a neighboring teenager to accompany him, and set off for the Congress. John caught up to the rest of the Massachusetts delegation at Hartford, and they all traveled on together from there.

This time the Congress met in the statehouse at Philadelphia, and a delegation from Georgia was present for the deliberations. The delegates from New England marveled at how different the issues facing them now were. The year before, the Congress had argued over what to do about the tea tax and a boycott of English goods was put in place. This time there were much more serious issues at hand. Should all of the colonies unite and go to war against England, or should they try to patch things up with the mother country?

It was a question to which John had only one answer—war or death! He encouraged the colonies to establish independent governments that could then band together into a formal confederation. Not everyone agreed with him. Many delegates could not imagine separating their colony from Great Britain.

After three weeks of haggling, the Continental Congress reached a compromise. A resolution was passed giving Massachusetts the right to govern itself until the British were willing to back off the tax issue and stop interfering in the appointment of their governor and judges.

While John had to content himself with this compromise for now, there was another issue he determined to push until he got his way. Congress decided to nominate a general to take command of the sixteen thousand militiamen who were now gathered around Boston. These men needed to be molded into an effective, professional army like the redcoats. There were two main contenders for the position. The first was John Hancock, who had been elected president of the second Continental Congress. Although he had never served in an army, he thought the job should be his because many of the fighting men were from his home colony of Massachusetts. The other contender was forty-three-year-old George Washington of Virginia, who had been a colonel in the militia for many years.

Although John Hancock was a fellow Bostonian and a friend, John Adams had no doubt that George Washington was the better man for the job.

Not only did Washington have experience and a commanding presence about him, but he was also from a southern colony. To John this was important because he wanted all the colonies to feel that they had a part to play in the army rather than just see it as something the people of Massachusetts were involved in. So, much to John Hancock's dismay, John Adams nominated George Washington to be the commander in chief of what was to be known as the Continental army. The Congress elected Washington unanimously.

John was pleased with the result, but he realized that for every decision the Congress made, ten more faced them. He was appointed chairman of twenty-five committees and served on thirty others! Each had its own set of players and its own issues and problems. John tried to put his feelings in a letter to Abigail:

> When fifty or sixty men have a constitution to form for a great empire, at the same time that they have a country of fifteen hundred miles in extent to fortify, millions to arm and train, a naval power to begin, and extensive commerce to regulate, numerous tribes of Indians to negotiate with, a standing army of twenty-seven thousand men to raise, pay, victual, and officer, I really shall pity those fifty or sixty men.

The courier who had been entrusted to carry the letter to Abigail was stopped at a British roadblock and searched. The letter was found and published in Boston. It caused an uproar, especially the words *constitution* and *naval power*. Many people had no idea that the Continental Congress was contemplating such things.

John knew he had used poor judgement in writing so openly to his wife, but he did not have time to dwell on it. Other, more important matters were presenting themselves. On Saturday, June 17, the day after General George Washington rode from Philadelphia to rally the troops, a battle broke out in Boston. On a peninsula across the Charles River from Boston lay Charlestown, with Bunker Hill and Breed's Hill rising behind the settlement. The patriots had decided that canons mounted on both these hills would give them a clear advantage over the British troops holed up in Boston. During the night patriot troops crept onto the peninsula and began building a fortification on Breed's Hill.

When the British awoke the following morning and saw colonial troops looking across the Charles River at them, they began firing on them from Copp's Hill in Boston and from various men-of-war at anchor in the harbor. A few hours later, fifteen hundred redcoats were put ashore at the bottom of Breed's Hill. With bayonets gleaming they charged up the hill. They were turned back twice by the patriot soldiers. But on their third attack they overran the colonial positions and took control of Breed's Hill, Bunker Hill, and the rest of Charlestown. It was a ferocious fight, however, and the British paid a heavy price for their victory. Rebel spies reported that 226 British soldiers had been killed in the fighting, and 2,400 were wounded. The casualties among the patriot militias had been 140 killed, 270 wounded, and 30 taken prisoner.

John and the other delegates heard the first sketchy news of the battle two days later. In the course of the briefing, John also learned the hard-to-believe news that his good friend Dr. Joseph Warren was dead. Dr. Warren had gone into the battle as a volunteer, and during the fighting a musket ball had hit the right side of his head, killing him instantly. This news was not only a personal blow to John but also a blow to the entire patriot cause. Dr. Warren was among the three or four most respected leaders in the movement, and a man of his caliber would be very difficult to replace.

A week later a letter arrived from Abigail by special courier, filling John in on more details. She had taken Johnny to the top of Penn's Hill in time to see the black smoke billowing over Charlestown. "The day; perhaps the decisive day is come on which the fate of America depends. My bursting heart must find vent in my pen," she wrote. She went on to describe the crushing loss of Dr. Warren. "He fell gloriously fighting for our country. Great is our Loss. The race is not to the swift, nor the battle to the strong, but the God of Israel is he that giveth strength and power unto his people. Trust in him at all times."

After receiving the letter, John wished he could go home and comfort Abigail and the children. It seemed that many of the other delegates were also feeling the need for a break, and so in August the Continental Congress recessed for a month. Many of the delegates from the southern colonies headed north to see the situation in Boston for themselves and to visit General Washington's camp.

On his way back to Braintree, John stopped in Cambridge to see the troops. As soon as he arrived, he saw that the army was in trouble. The enemy was not the redcoats but dysentery, an often fatal intestinal disease caused by lack of hygiene. Everywhere he looked, the scene was dreadful, with men doubled up in pain or vomiting. To make matters worse, John received a letter from Abigail informing him that his brother Elihu had just died of the disease. He quickly left Cambridge and hurried home.

The situation John returned to in Braintree was more difficult than when he had left. Every house in the town had one or two refugee families crammed into it. The family Abigail had taken in had two small children and a mother who was pregnant with a third. There was hardly a place to be alone in the house.

John marveled at how well Abigail handled everything. The summer had been particularly hot and dry, but she had managed to nurse the crops in the field to maturity.

While he was home, John took the opportunity to talk to sea captains. He was particularly interested in the idea of commissioning fishing boats and other commercial vessels to act as privateers, privately owned ships that were given permission to plunder enemy ships. As John talked to these men, he grew confident that privateers could be very useful to the American cause. They could capture much of the cargo meant for the British army and "redistribute" it to the fighting colonists.

John hated to have to leave his family again and return to the Continental Congress, though he knew it was his duty to do so. He feared there might be more deaths in the family, and there were. No sooner had he left than everyone in the house, including the servants and farmhands, came down with dysentery. Abigail's mother came to help out, and she, too, became ill. Within weeks of arriving back in Philadelphia, John got word that his mother-in-law and niece had died and that everyone else had been very ill. Like so many other delegates, he felt torn between the desire to be home with his grieving family and the need to stay and shape the future of the American colonies.

When John arrived back in Philadelphia in September 1775, everyone had lots of new ideas to discuss, but one issue remained unsolved. The delegates could not agree on a single course of action. Should they cut their ties with Great Britain, or should they continue to attempt reconciliation?

For John the question had been long answered, and he continued to imagine independent colonies with governments that represented their people and were linked together by a confederation. But he had no illusions that this would be easy to achieve. In fact, he wrote in his diary, "[T]he most difficult and dangerous part of business Americans have to do in this mighty contest, [is] to contrive some method for the colonies to glide insensibly from under the old government into a peaceable and contented submission to new ones."

By the word *insensibly,* John meant without pain or trauma. However, he was concerned that this might not happen. The American cause was not going well. Something else was needed to stir the colonists, but John did not know what that something was. But he did recognize it when he saw it. When John held in his hands a copy of Thomas Paine's booklet *Common Sense,* he knew it was something that could ignite the colonies and put America on the path to independence.

Although Thomas Paine was an English immigrant, John thought he understood the need for independence from Great Britain more than most of the delegates at the Continental Congress. Paine had set down these reasons in an easy-to-read manner in his booklet. He wrote:

> [To declare independence] may at first seem strange and difficult, but like all other steps which we have already passed over, will in a little time become familiar and agreeable; and until an independence is declared, the continent will feel itself like a man who continues putting off some unpleasant business from day to day, yet knows it must be done, hates to set about it, wishes it over, and is continually haunted by the thoughts of its necessity.

Common Sense was an instant success, selling more than 150,000 copies. As they read it, ordinary people began to understand what was at stake and urged their delegates to vote for independence. While this pleased John, it scared him as well. No one seemed to be thinking of what would happen *after* independence. In his opinion it was no use being free from Great Britain unless the people could come up with a fairer system by which to govern themselves. To help this process along, John set to work writing down his ideas in a pamphlet called *Thoughts on Government*.

This document brought together ideas that John had been thinking about for many years. It included the idea of three branches of government—the legislative, executive, and judicial branches—and the concept of a government ruled by laws and not by men. John ended his thoughts on an optimistic note, saying, "How few of the human race have ever enjoyed an opportunity of making an election of government...for themselves or their children! When, before the present epoch, had three millions of people full power and a fair opportunity to form and establish the wisest and happiest government that human wisdom can contrive?"

As *Common Sense* made its way through the colonies, people were ready to take on the British, and things began to move fast. In March, General Washington led an assault on the redcoats in Boston, and the British pulled their army out of the city!

The following month, the Continental Congress took John's advice and commissioned privateers. It also declared American ports open to trade with any country in Europe.

During this time John also received a startling letter from Abigail. When he had been home during the recess of the Congress, he had noticed that his wife was more self-assured than he had ever seen her before. He put this down to the fact that she now had to run the farm and was making many of the decisions that he normally would have made had he been there. But still, John was shocked and amused to read her advice to him:

> I long to hear that you have declared independency—and by the way in the new Code of Laws, which I suppose it will be necessary for you to make I desire you would remember the ladies, and be more generous and favorable to them than your ancestors. Do not put such unlimited power into the hands of the husbands. Remember all men would be tyrants if they could. If particular care and attention is not paid to the ladies, we are determined to foment a rebellion, and will not hold ourselves bound by any laws in which we have no voice, or representation.

John chuckled to himself as he read his wife's letter, and then he shot back a reply:

> As to your extraordinary Code of Laws, I cannot but laugh. We have been told that

> our struggle has loosened the bands of government every where. That children and apprentices were disobedient—that schools and colleges were grown turbulent—that Indians slighted their guardians, and Negroes grew insolent to their masters. But your letter was the first intimation that another tribe more numerous and powerful than all the rest were grown discontented.

After replying to Abigail's letter, John gave the idea of women's rights little more thought. The whole concept was such a strange new notion to him.

In May, the Congress passed a resolution advising each colony to set up its own representative government. John was pleased with this move, but he still thought the colonies needed to band together and formally declare their independence from Great Britain. This did not seem likely, however, and John despaired, saying, "You cannot make thirteen clocks strike precisely at the same second." The thirteen clocks he was referring to were, of course, the thirteen colonies, which never seemed to be headed in exactly the same direction at the same time.

Despite John's pessimism, on June 7, 1776, Virginia's Richard Henry Lee proposed "that the Congress should declare that these United Colonies are, and of right ought to be, free and independent states." John seconded the motion, but other delegates were not so sure. The men from New York, New Jersey, Delaware, and Pennsylvania wanted more time to think about such a daring move, and so the Congress delayed the vote on independence until July 1. In the meantime it appointed a five-man committee to look into the wording of such a document declaring independence. The five men appointed were Thomas Jefferson, Benjamin Franklin, Roger Sherman, Robert Livingston, and John Adams.

Other committees were set up, and John found himself on a committee that was to work out ways in which a new country could establish treaties with foreign powers. There was also a Board of War and Ordnance, which John was asked to chair.

John found himself in the midst of three very important tasks, any one of which could easily have taken up all his time. He forgot about socializing and set himself to work for eighteen hours a day. The time was short. He and the other delegates had less than three weeks to come up with a blueprint for a new nation.

Chapter 12

The Newborn Republic

John was up before dawn on Monday, July 1, 1776. After washing and dressing, he sat down and wrote a long letter to a friend and former delegate to the Continental Congress, Archibald Bulloch of Georgia. In his letter he wrote, "This morning is assigned the greatest debate of all. A declaration, that these colonies are free and independent states, had been reported by a committee some weeks ago for that purpose, and this day or tomorrow is to determine its fate. May heaven prosper the newborn republic."

Later that morning John set out for the statehouse. It was clear as he walked that it was going to be another hot and steamy day in Philadelphia.

At precisely ten o'clock the doors to the hall were closed, and John Hancock cracked the gavel on the table at the front where he sat presiding over the Congress's deliberations. "We are here to consider the motion of Richard Henry Lee of Virginia," he reminded the delegates.

After the full text of the motion was read, debate began. John Dickinson, a gaunt, pale member of the Pennsylvania delegation, stood. Dickinson, an opponent of independence, began to lay out reasons why declaring independence at this time was premature. There were no advantages to separating from England at this time, he asserted. Indeed, to declare independence might cause the British to throw off all restraint and cause greater calamity for the colonists of North America. "To proceed with a declaration of independence at this time is to brave the storm in a skiff of paper," Dickinson concluded before again taking his seat.

The room fell silent, and John Adams waited anxiously to see whether anyone would rise and speak in favor of independence. When no one did, John clambered to his feet. "I wish now, as never in my life, that I had the gifts of the ancient orators of Greece and Rome. I am certain none of them ever had before him a question of greater importance than that before this body," he began.

John went on to lay out the arguments he had made to the Congress many times before as to why independence from Great Britain was a good thing for America. To John's surprise he spoke more eloquently and passionately than he ever had before when giving a speech. He had no notes to follow; he simply followed his heart, which beat for independence.

As John was nearing the end of his speech, the door to the chamber swung open and in walked the delegates from New Jersey, who had just arrived in Philadelphia. They asked John to repeat what he had said so far so that they could be filled in on his argument. John obliged, and after standing to speak for two hours, he finally slumped back into his chair totally exhausted.

A thunderstorm had broken outside. As the wind whipped and the rain beat against the windows, the temperature inside the room began to cool down, making conditions a little more pleasant for everyone as the debate over independence continued on into the afternoon.

Finally, as the sun set over Philadelphia, a preliminary vote was taken to see just where the Congress stood on the issue. Four colonies voted against declaring independence. New York's citizens were so divided over the issue of independence that, as expected, the colony's delegation abstained from voting. Despite popular support for independence in Pennsylvania, the delegates from this colony had voted four to three against it. And since Caesar Rodney, one of the three delegates from Delaware, was sick and had not returned to the Congress, the two remaining delegates split their vote. Because a "yes" vote required a majority, this pushed Delaware into the "against" column. The surprise was South Carolina. Most people had thought this delegation supported independence, but surprisingly they had voted against it.

Although this gave independence a majority of the votes, the delegates at the Congress believed that such an important issue as independence ought to be passed unanimously, or at least as close to unanimously as possible. So instead of taking a final vote on whether or not to declare independence, one of the delegates moved that the Congress recess for the evening and the final vote be taken the following day. John thought this a wise idea, since it would allow the evening to be used to lobby and try to change the minds of those colonies and delegates that had voted against the measure.

The following morning, as John made his way back to the statehouse, he did not know what to expect. Had any minds been changed? He hoped so, but only time would tell. Like many of the other delegates, he had sat around at City Tavern the night before trying to convince the holdouts that independence was in the best interests of the American colonies.

As John waited for the session to begin, he was surprised when Caesar Rodney rather shakily made his way into the room and took his seat. Despite the fact that it was summer, Rodney had a green scarf wrapped around his head, covering a large cancerous lesion on the side of his face. John quickly learned that a messenger had been dispatched from Philadelphia after the preliminary vote the night before to find Rodney and bring him back for this morning's vote. On hearing what had happened, Rodney, a supporter of independence, had climbed out of his sickbed and ridden eighty miles through the night to get to Philadelphia in time for the vote.

Another surprise awaited John when John Hancock finally gaveled the meeting to order. The seats where John Dickinson and Robert Morris, two of the Pennsylvania delegates who had voted against independence, had sat were empty.

The final vote on independence was then taken. This time, with Caesar Rodney present, two of the three Delaware delegates voted in the affirmative, giving Delaware's support to independence. And with John Dickinson and Robert Morris not present, the majority of the remaining Pennsylvania delegation voted in favor of the measure. As expected, New York still abstained, and upon seeing that no other colony was voting against independence, South Carolina changed its vote from the day before.

"Resolved: That these United States are, and, of right ought to be, free and independent states; that they are absolved from all allegiance to the British crown, and that all political connexion between them, and the state of Great Britain is, and ought to be, totally dissolved," a voice intoned, announcing the result of the vote.

John could scarcely believe it. By a vote of twelve to zero, with one abstaining, the colonies had voted in favor of independence from Great Britain. Finally the colonies had embraced what he had believed for many years—that the future of America lay in separating from England.

That night John wrote Abigail a long letter. After telling her about the vote in favor of independence, he wrote:

> The second day of July 1776 will be the most memorable epoch in the history of America. I am apt to believe that it will be celebrated by succeeding generations as the great anniversary festival. It ought to be commemorated as the Day of Deliverance by solemn acts of devotion to God Almighty. It ought to be solemnized with pomp and parade, with songs, games, guns, bells, bonfires, and illuminations from one end of the continent to the other from this time forward forever more.

The following day Congress was back at work. Having voted for independence, they now needed to discuss and vote on the text of a declaration of independence that Thomas Jefferson had drawn up. The text Jefferson had written was read aloud, and throughout the day the delegates made changes. They deleted about twenty-five percent of the text, thinking it not applicable, or too emotive, or beside the point. In the end some eighty changes were made to the document. The following day, July 4, 1776, the Continental Congress approved the text of the Declaration of Independence.

John Hancock and Charles Thomson, the president and the secretary respectively of the Congress, affixed their signatures to the document, which was sent off to have a final handwritten, or engrossed, copy made to which all the delegates would later affix their signatures. The engrossed copy of the Declaration of Independence was ready on August 2, and John Adams along with the other delegates at the Continental Congress went forward and signed the document. John was aware as he signed his name that what he was doing would be considered treason by the British and that if for some reason he were to fall into their hands, he would probably be hanged.

Even though the colonies were excited about the signing of the Declaration of Independence, John knew, perhaps more than any other man in America, that hard times were ahead. As the chairman of the Board of War and Ordnance, he constantly received letters and documents outlining the way the war was going, and it was not good. To boost the number of soldiers they could field, the British had hired thousands of German soldiers, whom the Americans called Hessians.

Then, a month after the celebration of the Declaration of Independence died down, John received word that Admiral Lord Howe and ships loaded with redcoats had sailed into New York Harbor and assaulted Brooklyn. Outnumbered by more than two to one by the British, the American troops had been quickly overwhelmed and pushed back to the edge of the East River. They were saved from certain capture by the British when a storm blew in. On the night of August 29, as heavy rain pelted down and fog rose from the river, the

Continental army made a daring escape across the East River to Manhattan, where they awaited a further assault by the British.

Letters from home were just as distressing as the official communiqués about the fighting that John was receiving. Another smallpox epidemic was raging in Boston, and Abigail informed John that she had taken the entire family to the city to undergo inoculation. John's heart jumped when he read this. The process was still just as risky as it had been when he was inoculated twelve years before. He desperately wanted to go home to his family, but he could not. The newly independent country needed him. He settled for praying for his family every morning.

More letters came. Abigail reported that Nabby had over six hundred erupting sores over her body, making it impossible to lie or sit without severe pain. Four-year-old Tommy was very ill, too, and had been delirious for two days. The letters gradually became more positive, and everyone survived the ordeal, though Nabby was left with hundreds of pox scars.

On September 1, news reached the Congress in Philadelphia that Admiral Howe and his brother, General Richard Howe, wanted to stop the fighting and start talking. Apparently neither brother wanted any more bloodshed and thought they had a way to end the war.

But who should go to negotiate with them? Congress discussed the matter and voted to send three men—Benjamin Franklin, Edward Rutledge, and John Adams.

The men set out immediately, hoping that the British brothers had favorable terms to offer them. On September 11, 1776, they arrived at the stately Billopp House in Tottenville on Staten Island. But as the talks progressed, it became obvious to John and the other two men that the Howe brothers had nothing to offer except a promise from the king of pardon for any rebel who said he was sorry. There was nothing the Americans could accept as a means for resolving the conflict, and the meeting soon broke up.

John left with a heavy heart. He knew that the war would go on and many more lives would be lost on both sides. Four days after the meeting, on September 15, the British crossed the East River and began attacking the American troops holed up on Manhattan Island.

Before returning to Philadelphia, John took some time off to visit Braintree. He arrived home depressed and exhausted. Since Abigail had always been interested in politics, he told her about all the problems he was encountering. Because it was difficult to get soldiers to fight outside of their home colony or under the leadership of someone they did not know, enlistments were down. And a number of colonists, especially in New York and other northern colonies, had stayed loyal to the British. In fact, New York colony had furnished more soldiers for the British than it had for General Washington's army. But who could blame them, John lamented to his wife. Congress had no money to pay Continental soldiers and very few supplies to offer them.

Abigail listened patiently to John's problems and recited her woes to him as well. It was almost impossible to get anyone to help with the farm-work, and since her brother William had gone to sea on a privateer, she'd had his daughter Louisa to look after as well. And the new Continental money was hardly worth the paper it was printed on. She wondered how long it would be before people began to starve to death. John understood these problems, but there was little he could do about them, except listen and try to encourage Abigail.

John continued to receive word of how things were going on the battlefield. The Continental forces had been forced to flee Manhattan Island, with the British in close pursuit. General Howe and his troops chased Washington and his men all the way across New Jersey. Indeed, the British could easily have marched all the way to Philadelphia and captured the city, except that General Howe decided not to cross the Delaware River into Pennsylvania. Instead he set up winter camp for his redcoats in New Jersey.

And then some good news arrived. On the night of December 25, General Washington and five thousand ragtag troops had crossed the Delaware back into New Jersey and early the following morning attacked the British, catching them completely by surprise and taking nearly one thousand Hessian troops captive in the process. Then, on January 3, Washington made another surprise raid on the British at Princeton. Again the enemy was routed and prisoners were taken.

They were small victories, and the might of the British army was far from defeated, but to John, as to every other patriot in America, they were encouraging. They kept alive hope that the British could indeed be beaten.

On January 9, 1777, with great reluctance, John returned to the Continental Congress. Because an attack on Philadelphia by the British seemed imminent, Congress had moved to Baltimore. But the change of venue meant little to John; the same round of duties awaited him when he got there.

Abigail wrote soon after his arrival in Baltimore to say that she was expecting another baby. The news gladdened John's spirits, and he hoped that the new baby would be a girl to help take the place of Susanna and keep Abigail company.

The war continued. But to everyone's surprise, instead of crossing the Delaware River and beginning an assault on Philadelphia, Admiral Howe pulled his troops back to New York. Everyone waited anxiously to see where the British would attack next. Would they march up the Hudson River and try to cut New England off from the rest of the colonies, or would Howe load his troops onto ships and mount an attack somewhere to the south?

With no attack on Philadelphia impending, the Continental Congress moved back from Baltimore.

Throughout this time John often thought of Abigail and prayed that she was coping with all her tasks along with being pregnant. On July 23 a fleet of 260 British warships loaded with seventeen thousand troops sailed out of New York Harbor. An attack somewhere seemed imminent, but no one was sure where. That same day John received a letter from Braintree. He recognized the handwriting as that of his assistant, John Thaxter. With trembling hands he opened the letter and read.

> July 13
>
> Sir
>
> The day before yesterday Mrs. Adams was delivered of a daughter, but it grieves me to add, Sir, that it was still born. It was an exceeding fine looking child.
>
> Mrs. Adams is as comfortable...as can be expected; and has desired me to write a few lines to acquaint you that she is in a good way...

John put down the letter and wept. There was nothing else he could do.

On August 30 the British fleet was sighted off Cape May, at the entrance to Delaware Bay. It appeared that it intended to attack Philadelphia from the south. Tensions in Philadelphia were high as people waited to see when and how the British would attack them.

Like the other residents of the city, John breathed a sigh of relief when Washington and his Continental army marched through town on their way south to defend Philadelphia. For most of the inhabitants of the city, it was the first time they had laid eyes on the Continental army.

Washington's men took up position at Chadd's Ford, on Brandywine Creek, twenty-four miles south of Philadelphia, where they hoped to ambush the British who were marching north from the head of Chesapeake Bay, where they had been put ashore. However, Washington had miscalculated. There were other places apart from Chadd's Ford where the British could cross the river, and that is what they did. They crossed farther upstream and circled round behind the American troops to attack them. The Continental forces were soundly beaten, and Philadelphia lay unprotected.

Panic gripped the city. The members of the Continental Congress furiously gathered their papers together and fled to the city of York, one hundred miles to the west. Many residents of Philadelphia followed them in an exodus from the city. On September 26, the British took control of Philadelphia.

Washington mounted a counterattack against the British at Germantown, on the outskirts of Philadelphia, but the attack failed. A fog rolled in, and unable to see, the Continental soldiers began firing at each other instead of at the British and were forced to retreat.

It was a dismal time for John and the other members of Congress holed up in York. John began to have doubts about Washington's leadership of the Continental army and his ability to get the job done against the British.

Then in October came some good news from the battlefield. John's spirits soared as he read how

British General John Burgoyne and over five thousand redcoats who had been marching south from Quebec had surrendered to the American forces at Saratoga, New York.

By late fall 1777, John was well overdue for a break. Congress granted him an extended leave, and on November 7 he hurried back to Braintree. He was glad the war had taken a positive turn and happy at the thought of spending some time relaxing and getting to know his family again.

Back at home, John was content walking up Penn's Hill with ten-year-old Johnny and listening to his youngest son, five-year-old Tommy, repeat his alphabet. Suddenly the war seemed a long way away from him. After a few weeks he even took on a legal case as a favor to an old friend. It meant that he had to go to Portsmouth, New Hampshire, for two weeks, but John did not mind. He looked forward to being in a courtroom again. He left Abigail in a happy frame of mind, never for a moment guessing he would return to a distraught wife.

Chapter 13

A Commissioner to France

While John was in Portsmouth, word reached him that Congress had elected him to be a commissioner to France. John could hardly believe it—France! He spoke very little of the language and knew nothing of the customs of the country three thousand miles across the Atlantic from Massachusetts. In September 1776 Congress had appointed three men—Benjamin Franklin, Silas Deane, and Arthur Lee—to France as ambassadors for the colonies. Their job was to try to convince King Louis XVI to form an alliance with them and send men and supplies to help with the fighting in the American colonies. But things had not gone well, and an alliance with France still had not come about.

Benjamin Franklin, an old man of seventy-two, was barely able to keep up with the workload, and Silas Deane appeared to have taken the opportunity to line his own pockets rather than look out for the good of the American colonies. As a result, Deane was being recalled to answer questions, and John, well-known for his meticulous attention to paperwork, was to take his place. His most important task would be to speed along the alliance with King Louis XVI.

It was a freezing winter's day as John rode home to Braintree after two weeks away. He knew he would have to break the stunning news of his appointment to Abigail, and as he rode along, he wondered how he would do it. He was sure she would not like the news.

When he arrived home, John noticed that Abigail's face was red and swollen from crying. "What's the matter?" he asked, fearing one of the children had died while he was away.

"You got a packet of letters from Congress while you were gone. I thought they might contain something urgent, so I opened them." She picked up one letter and handed it to John. "I never dreamed it would say this."

John took the letter, though he already knew what it contained—confirmation of his appointment to France. He had no opportunity to soften the blow for Abigail; they were in for the longest separation of their lives.

"And a winter crossing of the Atlantic," Abigail said, tears now slipping down her cheeks. "It's so dangerous, and I might not see you for years. And if the British capture you, you'll be hanged. What are we to do, John?"

John slipped his arm around his wife and tried to comfort her. Even though neither of them was happy that the new appointment would keep them apart, they nonetheless would not entertain the idea of his turning it down. France's help was crucial to America's winning the war, and whatever sacrifices had to be made, the Adamses were willing to make them.

Abigail went straight to work collecting the things John would need for the voyage across the Atlantic, which could take up to eight weeks in winter. He would need to take his own bedding, food, and supplies. While Abigail sewed and preserved food, John wound up his business affairs. While he was in Congress, several of his clients had stayed with him, but now he advised them to find themselves a new lawyer.

There was no way the family could go with John. It was simply too dangerous a crossing for them all to undertake, but one member of the family had his heart set on accompanying him. Eleven-year-old Johnny begged his father to take him along. It was an agonizing decision for John and Abigail to make, but in the end they decided to let him go. A new country like America would need young men to become diplomats, and it seemed to them like a wonderful opportunity for Johnny to learn firsthand what this entailed.

John and Abigail often sat in silence through this time, thinking about what lay ahead for both of them. Finally, on February 13, 1778, news arrived that the twenty-four-gun Continental frigate *Boston* lay at anchor offshore from Mount Wolleston, where the family homestead in which Abigail's uncle, Norton Quincy, lived was located.

Abigail had already made it clear that she could not bear to see her husband and son climb aboard the ship, so the family said good-bye privately at their home in Braintree. At this time John gave his wife of fourteen years a locket he had bought in Boston. On it was painted a lone woman watching a ship sail away. It was inscribed with the words, "I yield whatever is is right."

John and his son climbed into a sleigh and headed over the snowy road to Mount Wolleston. They had sent most of their luggage, including two sheep, six live chickens, fourteen dozen eggs, a barrel of apples, and five bushels of corn, on ahead to Uncle Norton's house. John dared not look back as they left Braintree. He knew it would only make their parting more difficult for Abigail.

At Mount Wolleston they were met by a man named Joseph Stephens, who was going along to France as John's servant.

After dining with the *Boston*'s captain, Samuel Tucker, and Abigail's uncle, they were rowed out to the ship. However, the weather conditions were not right, and it was another thirty-six hours before the *Boston* finally got under way. But the ship made it only as far as Marblehead before it was forced to drop anchor. A heavy snowstorm blew in across western Massachusetts, reducing visibility to zero. For two days the ship sat at anchor as wind and driving snow swirled around it. Finally the storm broke, the winds turned favorable, and the *Boston* once again set sail. It made its way past the northern tip of Cape Cod and on out into the Atlantic Ocean.

The ocean off the coast of North America was patrolled by British warships, and from high in the mainmast a sailor kept vigilant watch of the horizon, searching for other ships. "Ships ahoy," he yelled to the captain several days out into the Atlantic.

John watched as Captain Tucker scanned the horizon with his telescope. Sure enough, coming up behind them were three British men-of-war. The captain began barking orders to his crew to set more sail and try to get more speed to outrun the British ships.

The *Boston* plowed through the icy water of the Atlantic. John watched anxiously as the British ships drew closer, but Captain Tucker managed to keep his ship ahead. Finally, after two days, two of the British ships began to fall behind and broke off the pursuit. But the largest of the three ships kept following them.

John began to be concerned when it looked like the lone British ship was gaining on them. He had with him many important official documents from

Congress—documents he could not let fall into the hands of the British. So he began making plans in case the British man-of-war caught up with the *Boston* and boarded it.

John loaded all his documents into a trunk and threw a cast-iron weight into it. He lashed the trunk to the deck, ready to be cut free and thrown overboard at a moment's notice. And John, too, was ready to throw himself overboard into the frigid Atlantic if he had to. As a traitor to King George III, he could expect no mercy.

Captain Tucker used all his skill as a sailor to keep the *Boston* ahead, but the British man-of-war was never far behind. John kept watch anxiously, looking to see if the British were gaining on them.

As the sun began to set on the third day of the pursuit, a howling storm blew up. The surface of the Atlantic, always turbulent at this time of year, became violent. Huge waves whipped by the wind smashed over the ship. Captain Tucker ordered the crew to furl the sails and take the passengers below.

Below deck John and his son lay on their bunks trying to stop themselves from being flung about as the *Boston* pitched and rolled erratically. By now they were both violently seasick. To make matters worse, as the huge, froth-crested waves washed across the deck, water seeped below, drenching everything.

The following day as John clung to his bunk, he heard a mighty crack and felt the ship shudder. He wondered what it was, and eventually his curiosity got the better of him. He stumbled up on deck to find the mizzenmast split from top to bottom. The *Boston* had been struck by lightning near where three sailors were standing. Two of them, who would recover, had been taken below. The body of a third sailor still lay on the deck where he had fallen. John looked closely. He had never seen anything like it before. The lightning bolt had blown a hole in the man's skull.

After two days of lashing the ship, the storm abated, and John came back on deck to survey the damage. The crew was already busy making repairs. And there was a lot to repair. Destruction was everywhere. Rigging and broken pieces of yardarms were strewn about the deck. Smashed barrels and crates, their contents spilled, lay everywhere. John had to be careful where he placed his feet lest he trip on some piece of wreckage as he walked over to Captain Tucker, who was scanning the horizon with his telescope. "What about the British?" he asked." Are they still pursuing us."

"Nowhere to be seen," the captain replied. "I expect they're putting themselves back together again, just like us. I think we've seen the last of them for a while."

"I hope you're right," John replied.

The captain was right; they never spotted the British man-of-war again. The weather improved too, and they enjoyed many days of plain sailing.

Captain Tucker took a shine to Johnny, and after repairs to the ship were made, he regaled him with stories of life at sea. While the captain was only thirty years old, he had gone to sea when he was eleven, the same age as Johnny. Since that time he had visited many exotic ports of call and lived through many harrowing experiences. Johnny sat transfixed, soaking up all that the captain had to say.

Meanwhile John struck up a friendship with Dr. Nicholas Noel, a French surgeon who, along with a group of his fellow countrymen, was returning to France on the *Boston* after helping fight the British. Dr. Noel was a well-educated man who spoke impeccable English and tried to help John with his French.

Finally, in mid-March, land was sighted. They were in the Bay of Biscay on the north coast of Spain. Through a telescope John could see the snowcapped mountains of northern Spain.

The *Boston* plowed on and began making its way up the southwest coast of France. Finally, on March 30, the ship entered the Gironde, where a pilot came aboard to guide them upriver to Bordeaux. As they moved along, John stood transfixed on deck staring at the amazing countryside. It was different from anything he had ever seen before. He wrote in his journal, "Europe, thou great theater of arts, sciences, commerce, war, am I at last permitted to visit thy territories?"

On March 31, 1778, the *Boston* anchored at Bordeaux, and several of the passengers were invited to dine on a nearby French ship. There, with Dr. Noel acting as interpreter, John learned an astonishing fact. The alliance he had been sent to work on was already signed. In fact, it had been signed on February 6, a week before John left Braintree. Still, there was little John could do about that now, so he decided to travel on to Paris and make himself useful in other ways.

On April 4 he and Johnny began their journey to Paris, pushing to cover a hundred miles a day. They reached their destination on April 8. Benjamin Franklin greeted John warmly.

It soon became obvious how difficult it was to find suitable accommodations in Paris. John accepted Franklin's offer to stay with him at Passy, one of the outer suburbs of Paris and not far from the weekday boarding school that John enrolled Johnny in. Two of Franklin's grandsons went to the school as well, and much to John's relief, Johnny fit right in. He did not even complain about the fencing and dance lessons he had to take.

With Johnny happily settled into school, John set to work to find out what shape the American Commission to Paris was in. He was in for a shock! No one had kept accurate books on the money flowing in and out of the commission. Nor were there copies of any of the official letters that had been written. The only thing Benjamin Franklin appeared to take seriously was his dinner date book, which was completely full. From John's viewpoint he lived much more like a French nobleman than a patriot sent to represent a revolution.

John set to work to impose order on the chaos he had uncovered. However, he soon learned that no one else was very interested in his ideas. Benjamin Franklin and Arthur Lee could not agree on anything. They even argued bitterly about the Fourth of July celebration that the commission was sponsoring that year. And to make matters worse, everyone was sure there were British spies among the commission staff, which made it difficult to get any planning done.

Eventually John came to the conclusion that the situation was hopeless. He and Benjamin Franklin and Arthur Lee were all working at cross-purposes, promising the same money to different people and signing agreements that contradicted each other. He wrote to Samuel Adams, recommending that Congress replace all the commissioners, including himself, with one minister. He also urged that Congress give that minister strict allowances and expense accounts and require him to keep a letter book, an account book, and a minute book.

In the midst of all this, France finally declared war on Britain and made a firm commitment to be an ally of the American colonies.

In early 1779 word finally reached John that Congress had taken his advice—to a point. A letter arrived announcing the disbanding of the commission and appointing Benjamin Franklin as the sole minister to France, while Arthur Lee was dispatched to Madrid, Spain. John, though, was not mentioned at all in the letter. He could hardly believe it. What was he supposed to do now? And how could Congress be so careless as to not give instructions to one of their commissioners?

All of this made John feel very depressed and, coupled with the fact that it took three months for a letter to arrive from America, made him want to go home.

By March 1779 John had still not heard anything about a new appointment, so he decided that home to Braintree was where he would go. John and twelve-year-old Johnny, along with Joseph Stephens, climbed aboard the *Sensible* for the return voyage. The voyage home was uneventful compared to the voyage to France, and after a seven-week passage, they arrived back on American soil near Braintree. It was August 2, a beautiful summer's day. Since no one was expecting them, Johnny ran up to Uncle Norton's house to get someone to help with their luggage.

After depositing the three passengers ashore, the *Sensible* sailed northward to Boston, where it was headed for refurbishing. John had no idea that he would be back on board the ship in only three months' time!

Chapter 14

Peace at Last

When John finally reached Braintree later that day, he was glad to find Abigail and his two younger sons in good health. Nabby was in Boston, staying with Abigail's relatives, and a servant was dispatched to bring her home. Six-year-old Tommy was a little shy at first. After all, his father had been away for eighteen months. But he soon warmed to John and showed him the little American flag Abigail had bought him. The flag had thirteen stars and thirteen stripes on it to represent the thirteen colonies that had banded together to become one republic.

John was delighted with Tommy, and everything else around him. Abigail had done a wonderful job of running the farm, and Charles had grown into a responsible nine-year-old.

The only thing that bothered John on his return home was news of the war. In the spring of 1778, George Washington's army had emerged from their brutal winter encampment at Valley Forge a much more disciplined and able fighting force. They had proved that if nothing else they could hold their own against the British. After capturing and occupying Philadelphia, the British eventually abandoned the city and retreated to New York. And now, with Washington's troops surrounding New York, the war had reached a sort of stalemate. The British made small coastal raids up and down the coast of North America, but there had been no decisive battles that would turn the tide of the war in anybody's favor.

No matter how much John thought he could stay away from politics, his sense of public duty called him back. He had been in Braintree only a week when he was elected to the Massachusetts constitutional convention. This group of men had been picked to write a constitution for the colony so that it could become a self-governing state. John knew more about the topic than almost anyone else elected to the convention, and he felt obliged to help the others. Besides, he had already given so much for his colony that he wanted to see it standing firmly on its own feet.

Being part of the constitutional convention did not stop John from reopening his law practice, and by fall the harvest from the farm was in. John felt everything was running along just the way he wanted it to.

It was then that he received a letter from Philadelphia announcing that he had been chosen by Congress to return to France as the negotiator for peace with Great Britain. Of course the letter pointed out that the American colonies and Great Britain were still at war, but Congress hoped that America would soon win, and they wanted to have a minister a stone's throw away ready to negotiate when that happened. The task ahead of John would be a difficult one: He would be brokering peace agreements and commercial treaties. Despite the difficulty of the task, John knew right away he would accept the position.

This time John was traveling as a minister and not as a commissioner, and this made all the difference. His salary would be twenty-five hundred pounds, enough to comfortably live on, and he was allowed an official secretary as well as a servant.

John and Abigail pondered whether Johnny should go back to Europe with his father. Johnny spoke perfect French, and Abigail agreed that the French school had done wonders for his education. After a lot of soul searching, John and Abigail decided that not only should Johnny return to France but nine-year-old Charles should go as well.

Once again the Adams house was a flurry of activity. Much to Abigail's relief, John Thaxter offered to go along as John's private secretary and tutor for the boys, while Congress appointed Francis Dana to be John's official secretary. In addition,

Joseph Stephens agreed to make the return journey to Europe as John's servant.

Boxes that had not yet been unpacked were opened and their contents aired before being repacked for the return voyage. On November 15, 1779, the six-man party boarded the *Sensible*. They joined 340 other passengers making the early winter crossing to Europe. John was given the same cabin he had occupied on the voyage home, though this time he shared it with Charles, who would not stop crying for his mother. Johnny bunked in another cabin with John Thaxter.

Just as before, John had no idea how long he would be away. It all depended on how long it took for the war to end and, of course, on the hope that America won it. If not, John would become one of the most hunted men in Europe.

The voyage went well for the first weeks, and then things began to go very wrong. A severe storm engulfed the ship, battering it with howling winds and high seas. Finally, when the storm abated, it was discovered that the *Sensible* had sprung a leak. As each day passed, the leak got worse, until finally two pumps were set up to keep the ship from sinking. Passengers and crew worked busily around the clock to keep the pump going. But with the leak the ship was in no condition to outrun any British frigates it might come upon, and the captain told John that they would make for the closest port as fast as they could. There the leak could be repaired so that the ship could travel on to its destination of Brest, France.

The closest port was El Ferrol, on the rocky northwest coast of Spain. On December 8 the *Sensible* limped into port and dropped anchor. Paris lay one thousand miles to the northeast. When John learned it could take a month or longer to repair the leaking ship, he decided to set out overland for Paris. Many of the locals urged him not to do this, as it was an arduous trip at the best of times but in winter would be cold and miserable and there would be snow on the mountain trails. But John was undeterred; he could not sit around doing nothing for weeks while the *Sensible* was repaired.

As the sun rose on December 15, 1779, John and his party set out for Paris. Two passengers from the *Sensible,* also on their way to Paris, accompanied them, and two Spanish guides were employed to see them safely to the border with France. They rode on mules and stopped to stock up on provisions at the nearby town of La Coruña. They traveled eastward across northern Spain to Bilbao. The weather was cold and wet and foggy, and soon everyone in the group had a cold and a cough. In his journal John wrote, "We go along barking and sneezing and coughing as if we were fitter for a hospital than for travelers on the road."

From Bilbao the trail became even narrower and more treacherous than it already was. John had never seen such rugged, rocky mountains. They seemed to go on and on, and John referred to them as a "tumbling sea." In many places the trail was now so narrow and steep that they had to dismount from their mules and walk. It was bitter cold, and John began to regret making the decision to travel to Paris overland. But it was too late to go back, and they kept pushing on.

Finally, in mid-January 1780, they crossed the border into France at Saint-Jean-de-Luz. The trial of crossing the Pyrenees Mountains was behind them. They traveled to Bayonne, where they switched to riding in a carriage. On February 9 they arrived in Paris, travel weary and ready for a rest.

After such a harrowing trip, the arrival in Paris was an anticlimax. Johnny and Charles were sent off to boarding school during the week, and John spent his days trying to get permission to do his diplomatic work. This proved difficult because John had been instructed to work with the French foreign minister, Comte de Vergennes. The French, however, were understandably not eager for the fledgling united colonies in North America to negotiate commercial treaties with England when peace came. The French wanted the British to be isolated from world trade, giving them the upper hand.

All this proved to be one big headache. Wherever John went, he was entangled in red tape, and the French wanted it that way. In frustration he began writing to Congress every day, keeping them up-to-date with what was going on in France. This was really Benjamin Franklin's job, but John was so desperate for something useful to do that he did not care. However, when word reached Franklin that John was writing to Congress and to Comte de Vergennes, he was furious. He refused to entertain John anymore and turned his back on him when he came to visit.

By June of 1780, John had had enough of Paris. Just like last time, he had nothing useful to do, so he took his sons on an extended trip to the Netherlands. When Congress heard he was headed there, they appointed him to try to negotiate some Dutch loans for America, since Henry Laurens, the American minister to the Netherlands, was still in the United States.

On his way back to the Netherlands, however, Henry Laurens was captured at sea by the British and taken to England, where he was locked up in the Tower of London. Not only had the British captured Laurens, but they had been able to seize the official documents he was carrying before they could be destroyed. Among the captured documents was the text of a proposed treaty between the United States and the Netherlands. This created an outcry in London, since the Netherlands already had a treaty allying it with Britain! Orders were given to British naval captains to attack Dutch ships, and Europe was in an uproar. The war that had been raging in America for five years now began to engulf Europe. And John Adams found himself in Holland, right in the middle of all the tension. It took all his diplomatic skills to keep the Dutch government ministers and bankers sympathetic to the plight of the United States.

Meanwhile John was receiving regular reports from Congress about the course of the war, and what he read depressed him. Charleston had fallen to the British, and General Gates had been stunningly defeated by the British at Camden, South Carolina. The American southern army was in tatters as a result of the defeat. And as if this were not enough, one of the Continental army's prominent generals, Benedict Arnold, had committed treason and conspired with the British.

Letters from Braintree were no cheerier than news of the war. Abigail wrote to tell John of two deaths in the family—his brother Peter's wife, from complications in childbirth, and his stepfather, John Hall. And in a morbid frame of mind, Abigail had added that his mother bid him well but never expected to see him again.

While all this was happening, John was facing a big decision. His secretary, Francis Dana, had been commissioned by Congress to go to St. Petersburg, Russia, on a diplomatic mission. His task was to persuade the Russian empress, Catherine the Great, to recognize American independence.

Catherine the Great's court spoke French, and Francis Dana needed a secretary who could speak that language fluently. He asked John if his son Johnny, or John Quincy, as most people now called him, could accompany him in that capacity. John was not sure what to say. After all, John Quincy was only fourteen years old. If something happened to Francis Dana, his son would be twelve hundred miles away, alone in a land few English-speaking people had ever been to.

In the end the thought of all the new experiences John Quincy would encounter won out, and

John gave his permission. But allowing John Quincy to go to Russia brought John's problem with his next son into sharp focus. Charles, who had been homesick during the entire trip, was distraught at losing his big brother, and John could not console him. In the end he decided it was best to return Charles to Massachusetts on the first available ship. Now, with his family scattered across two continents and the wild ocean between them, John prayed that everyone would stay safe from harm.

Then, on November 23, 1781, John received some wonderful news. Finally the war had gone the Americans' way. Trapped by a combined French and American force on the York Peninsula in Virginia, British General Cornwallis had surrendered his army of over seven thousand men to George Washington at Yorktown. This was a quarter of all the British fighting forces in North America, and John was sure that such a defeat would break the British will to keep fighting. As news of the Americans' victory at Yorktown spread, attitudes began to change. The Dutch government, seeing that the British were beaten, officially recognized the United States in October 1782. It was the culmination of John's work in the Netherlands, and soon afterwards, John returned to France.

As John had thought, the British had grown tired of a war they could not seem to win and now wished to make peace. So when John arrived back in Paris, he found Benjamin Franklin and John Jay, who had just arrived from the United States, beginning negotiations for a peace treaty with the British. John was reluctant to meet with Franklin again, but both men had the sense to put their past differences behind them for the good of their new country. Besides, there were so many issues to address that it would take all three men working hard to deal with them all. They had to address such matters as American merchants who had owed debts to England before the war and now claimed that the war had canceled them out. And there were questions about how to compensate British loyalists in America who'd had their property taken away during the war and about what the British should do about the money and slaves they took from the plantation owners in the South. There were also questions about fishing rights off Newfoundland and about the western boundary of the United States.

John was very surprised at how easily the British negotiators gave in to the Americans' demands. Evidently the years of war had exhausted them, and they just wanted to get the whole business behind them.

It was a proud moment for John Adams, Benjamin Franklin, and John Jay when on September 3, 1783, the three of them signed the Treaty of Paris. The first sentence of the treaty read, "His Britannic Majesty acknowledges the said United States...to be free, sovereign and independent states." John watched as King George III's representative, David Hartley, signed on behalf of the king. With the stroke of a pen, the British now officially recognized an independent United States of America.

After the signing of the treaty, John's thoughts turned toward home. His job in Europe was over, or so he thought. However, the next batch of official papers from Congress said otherwise. Now that the United States was recognized as a nation, a whole new round of work had to be done in Europe. Twenty European states were clamoring for commercial treaties, and John was the obvious choice to negotiate them. But while he was prepared to do this, John secretly hoped that the position of the first United States ambassador to Great Britain might one day be his.

John put thoughts of going home out of his mind and got to work. But when Abigail wrote to say that her father had died and that Nabby was embroiled in a love affair with a questionable young man, John urged them both to join him in Paris. Abigail wrote back saying she would come as soon as she had put all the family business affairs in good hands. She planned to send Charles and Thomas to stay with her younger sister Elizabeth, who had recently married the Reverend John Shaw. And she planned to bring a maid and a butler with her to Paris.

While John waited for his wife and daughter to arrive, he worked on an endless round of treaties and negotiations. John Quincy returned safely from Russia, though he had made the dangerous return journey alone. John thought his son was quite grown up now, and he had kept up with his studies. John Quincy spoke French, Latin, Greek, and Dutch. The only subject he was weak in was arithmetic, and John began to tutor him in this subject in the evenings.

Finally, in early July 1784, John received a letter saying that Abigail and Nabby and their servants had made it to London and were waiting for him to collect them from there. Since he was in the middle of a particularly difficult negotiation, he sent John Quincy on ahead, promising to follow as soon as he could.

On August 17 John and Abigail were reunited after four years and nine months apart. John hardly recognized Nabby, who had grown into a tall young woman with her hair piled high on her head. But Abigail was just as he remembered her. He laughed when she told him that the state of the galley on the ship was so deplorable she had scrubbed the whole thing out herself and then set to making puddings for the crew and passengers. Even though she was traveling to Europe to be reunited with her diplomat husband, she saw no reason to forget her New England roots.

The family left England and traveled to France. As they crossed the English Channel toward Calais, John hoped he would be returning soon as ambassador to Great Britain.

Chapter 15

Vice President

John's hopes were realized eight months later when he received word that he was indeed going to be the first United States minister to Great Britain. A strange mix of emotions swirled in him as he, Abigail, and Nabby packed up their belongings and set out for London. John Quincy was not with them; he had returned to Cambridge to attend Harvard University, as his father had.

One of John's first duties after his arrival in London was to pay his respects to King George III. It was a strange meeting. John had to bow when he entered the king's bedchamber, as the room where the king held official meetings was called. He also had to bow when he got halfway across the marble floor, and again as he approached the king. With all the bowing over, the king fixed his eyes on John.

"The United States of America have appointed me their minister plenipotentiary to Your Majesty," John said, trying to keep the emotion out of his voice. He was well aware that he was standing before the ruler who only a few years before had declared John and the other members of the Continental Congress traitors and worthy of being hanged. Conversely, John and the Congress had labeled the king a tyrant who was unfit to be the ruler of a free country. And now they were standing face-to-face on equal terms, a New England lawyer turned diplomat, and the king of the most powerful nation on earth.

John stood for a long moment, grateful that he had memorized the speech he was about to deliver. "The appointment of a minister from the United States to Your Majesty's Court will form an epoch in the history of England and of America," he began. "I think myself more fortunate than all my fellow citizens, in having the distinguished honor to be the first to stand in Your Majesty's royal presence in a diplomatic character; and I shall esteem myself the happiest of men if I can be instrumental in recommending my country more and more to Your Majesty's royal benevolence, and of restoring an entire esteem, confidence, and affection, or, in better words, the old good nature and the old good humor between people who, though separated by an ocean and under different governments, have the same language, a similar religion, and kindred blood."

King George III smiled and nodded. Then he replied, welcoming John to England and expressing his happiness that John had been chosen to be the United States' minister to Great Britain. His voice was high and squeaky, and he spoke with a stutter, but he still managed to sound sincere. The king ended with a confession: "I will be very frank with you; I was the last to consent to separation; but the separation having been made, and having become inevitable, I have always said, as I say now, that I would be the first to meet the friendship of the United States as an independent power."

The two men spoke for a few more minutes, and then the king bowed, signaling to John that the interview was over. John bowed again and then, walking backwards so that he would not turn his back to the king, made his way out of the royal bedchamber, bowing twice more as he exited.

John was very pleased with the way his audience with the king had gone. He felt sure that the king was sincere in his promises to do all he could to bring England and the United States together as friends and trading partners. However, this was not entirely up to the king. The prime minister and Parliament had to be persuaded as well. Here matters did not go so well.

Many people in England and Europe believed that it was only a matter of time before the United States collapsed and came hat-in-hand back to England asking to be recognized as colonies again. This belief caused Parliament to drag its heels on every part of the Treaty of Paris. John pushed and pushed for them to honor their portion of the treaty, but he was met with many rebuffs. Not that the Americans were holding up their end of the treaty either. The Treaty of Paris said that colonies had to repay debts to England that they had entered into in good faith before the war, but several of the colonies had voted to ignore these debts. Once again John found himself soothing emotions and urging both sides to act honorably.

While he was hard at work doing this, the United States Congress was quickly running out of money, and it assigned John the difficult task of returning to the Netherlands to beg for loans. John made several such trips, each time joining forces with his friend Thomas Jefferson, who had been appointed as the United States' minister to France.

Meanwhile twenty-year-old Nabby had fallen in love with Colonel William Smith, a New Yorker who had been sent to England to act as secretary to the American delegation. John and Abigail approved of the match, and the young couple were married in a quiet ceremony at Grosvenor Square, London, on June 12, 1786. In a twist of fate, Nabby now became Abigail Smith, which was her mother's maiden name. Abigail's father, brother, and son-in-law all shared the name William Smith.

Abigail's sister Mary Cranch wrote to confirm that all three of the Adams boys were now studying at Harvard. Thankfully, the government had given them scholarships in honor of John's work on behalf of the country. Other family news was not so good, however. Abigail's brother William had disappeared with "bad company," leaving his wife and children to fend for themselves.

And from as far away as London, John could see that the new country was in trouble. The newly independent states did not want to work together. They taxed each other for everything that was sold across a state's border. The states were also bickering over who got which piece of western land captured from France in the Seven Years War and that Great Britain had agreed to hand over in accordance with the Treaty of Paris. Big states like Virginia thought they deserved a lot of this land, while the smaller states fretted that the larger ones were getting too large.

Then, in March 1786, Shays's Rebellion took place. In western Massachusetts farmers were furious over the high taxes they were forced to pay. Many of them, faced with selling their land to pay the taxes, decided to do something about it. A man named Daniel Shays led twelve hundred farmers, pitchforks in hand, in a violent protest. The farmers shut down the courts, emptied the debtors' prisons, and disrupted land auctions. Eventually four thousand militiamen were sent in to calm things down. Four protesters were killed in the bloody conflict.

John knew that the future of the new country lay in the former colonies' banding together to act as one. He wrote many letters home trying to help members of Congress as they sought to form a new government. The letters he received back suggested that the states would soon be ready to vote for a president and a vice president. George Washington was the strong favorite to become president; he was a war hero and an imposing figure in politics. But who would fill the position of vice president was not so clear. Most congressmen agreed that the position should go to a northerner—or Yankee, as they were now called—since Washington was a southerner and keeping a balance between the states was viewed as very important.

John wondered whether he had a chance at becoming vice president. After all, he had been involved in politics since the founding of the country, and he admired George Washington immensely. He made a few discrete inquiries, and sensing that his chances at being elected were good, he resigned his diplomatic post and prepared to return home.

Nabby and William Smith decided to return to America as well. Nabby had borne John and Abigail's first grandson, William Steuben Smith, in April 1787, and the young couple was anxious to set up home in New York.

Just before he and Abigail were due to set sail, John received word that a large house in northern Braintree that he had always admired was for sale. The owner was a loyalist who had fled to England during the war, leaving the house empty. John wrote to Abigail's uncle, Cotton Tufts, asking him to buy the house for them. It would be a fitting new home for the Adams family upon their return.

The same batch of mail that carried news of the house contained the sad news that Abigail's brother William had died.

John and Abigail and their two American servants, who were now married and expecting a baby, sailed from Cowes, England, on April 20, 1788, aboard the *Lucretia*. Strong winds kept the ship from making much headway, and they did not leave sight of England until the beginning of May.

Fifty-two-year-old John was on the way back to his homeland, where he had spent only a few months during the past ten years.

The crossing of the Atlantic was rough, but finally, on Tuesday, June 17, the *Lucretia* approached Boston Harbor. John and Abigail were expecting a modest welcome with a few family members and friends coming to meet them, but they were greeted with something quite different. As the *Lucretia* sailed past the lighthouse ten miles out from Boston, the lighthouse keeper signaled ahead that the Adamses were coming, and a cannon boomed out a salute from the fort at Castle Island.

By the time the ship had made her way into Boston Harbor and dropped anchor, thousands of Bostonians were gathered on the docks. Everyone waved and cheered as John and Abigail stepped ashore. John Hancock, who was now the governor of Massachusetts, had a coach waiting to take them to a huge reception at his Beacon Hill home. And church bells rang all day and into the night welcoming John. It was all quite overwhelming for him. He was not used to being applauded so publicly.

As soon as they could, John and Abigail slipped away from Boston and returned to Braintree, where they had a wonderful reunion with John's mother and with their three sons. John Quincy had finished college and gone into a law practice, where he was working toward being admitted to the bar in Boston. Eighteen-year-old Charles and fifteen-year-old Thomas were having a great time at Harvard. A little too much fun, John thought as he listened to their stories. He wished they had John Quincy's drive to study and learn, but they both appeared to be happy to barely scrape through their classes.

The house John had bought needed a lot of repairs and, at Abigail's insistence, redecorating. Soon John was living amidst a bustle of carpenters, artisans, and craftsmen, all being expertly guided by his wife into producing replicas of the latest Paris designs. They renamed the house Peacefield because it reminded John of the peace treaty he had signed with England and because he hoped it would be a peaceful place for him and Abigail to grow old in.

John found great joy in turning the eighty acres of land around Peacefield back into a productive farm. He mended fences, bought cows and sheep, and collected cartloads of seaweed to enrich the soil. But other, larger matters took up much of his time. He had to reacquaint himself with American politics and politicians. Many of John's old friends from Congress had either retired or died. Of the original fifty-six signers of the Declaration of Independence, fourteen were now dead.

In September 1788 John allowed his name to be put on the ballot for vice president. Congress had developed a complicated system whereby electors voted on behalf of their districts but did not have to vote the way their districts wanted them to. What's more, the person with the most votes got to be president and the person who came in second became the vice president. This meant that the president and the vice president could have opposite ideas on all sorts of issues but be forced to work together as a team.

It would have been unseemly for John to campaign for himself, but he took an avid interest in the outcome of the vote as the time for it drew closer. Abigail went to New York, then the capital city of the United States, to visit Nabby and help with the birth of her second child. It was another boy, whom they named John Adams Smith.

While she was in New York, Abigail took notes on all the political gossip so she could relay it to John. As best she could make out, she told John, he would win the vice presidency. Her assessment turned out to be correct. In March John learned that he was indeed going to be the first vice president of the United States of America, serving under President George Washington.

John left immediately for New York amid great fanfare. Cheering people lined the route, and wherever he stopped, he was greeted with official welcomes and presentations. Abigail stayed behind to pack up the house and wind up their affairs yet again.

When John arrived at the bridge leading to Manhattan Island and New York City, a troop of New York cavalry and an escort of congressmen on horseback met him. It was a proud moment for him, as was George Washington's swearing-in ceremony on Thursday, April 30, 1789. John stood on the balcony of Federal Hall beside the man whom fourteen years before he had nominated to lead the Continental army. As Washington repeated the oath of office, John thought back on all the trials the United States had come through and the many more that lay ahead. He silently prayed that he would be up to the task of helping guide the young nation forward.

It was not long before John began wondering whether he had any role to play at all in the new government. The constitution, which had been ratified ten months earlier, stated that the vice president was not to take part in any debates. Instead he was to chair the debates. He was not to vote in Congress unless there was a tie, in which case he was the one who would cast the deciding vote.

This was not easy for John. All his life he had liked to debate issues and share his knowledge with others, and now he had to keep silent on the very issues that affected the future of the country. He wrote to Abigail about what he thought of the office of vice president: "My country in its wisdom contrived for me the most insignificant office that ever the invention of man contrived or imagination conceived."

In June 1789 Abigail joined John in New York, and they moved into a large house at Richmond Hill, a mile and a half outside New York. Charles and Thomas came to live with them, and Nabby and William and their two little boys lived nearby.

Only John Quincy stayed in Boston, where he had passed the bar and was now a lawyer.

John was one of the few men in Congress who had ever been out of the United States. Even George Washington had been overseas only once, to accompany his older half brother to Barbados when he was dying with smallpox. Because of his experience as a foreign diplomat, John felt that for the United States to be taken seriously, its government would have to have a certain amount of pomp and ceremony. This did not sit well with some of the congressmen who had fought so hard to separate themselves from the "old world" of Europe.

The difference in opinion as to how formal the government should be was a major frustration to John. The debate over how to address the president raged on for over a month. Some, including John, wanted him addressed as "His Majesty the President," while others thought "Excellency" or "Sir" was more fitting. And John, who was used to seeing kings seated on their thrones, thought that the president should at least have a special ceremonial chair with a canopy over it.

Then there were issues of how Congress should act around the president. Should they sit or stand when he addressed them, and would the vice president chair the debates even when the president was in the room?

Another nagging question was where the permanent capital city should be. New York's congressmen assumed it would stay in New York and had already commissioned a presidential mansion to be built by the harbor. Pennsylvania's representatives thought it should be moved back to Philadelphia, while George Washington wanted a new capital city to be built somewhere along the Potomac River in his home state of Virginia.

A more serious division was also taking shape. The congressmen were quickly separating into two groups: the Federalists, who wanted a strong and powerful central federal structure governing all the states; and the Anti-Federalists, who wanted the individual states to have most of the power, with the central government having little control over them. John favored the Federalist position, but he felt he should not make his views widely known because his job was to support President Washington's opinions, not have his own.

As John was growing weary of all the arguing over these issues, a new and unexpected topic arose in Congress. In September word reached America that France was in the middle of its own bloody revolution. Many members of Congress were elated, seeing the revolution as common French men and women rising up to overthrow a corrupt monarchy. John saw it differently; he took it as a warning of what citizens could do if they felt their government was not acting in their interests. He wrote to Samuel Adams about his concerns for France. "Everything will be pulled down. So much seems certain. But what will be built up? Are there any principles of political architecture?... Will the struggle in Europe be anything other than a change in imposters?"

John had a feeling that the French Revolution had the potential to divide the new government as nothing else had before, and he read every newspaper and letter he could on the subject. He also talked a lot with Thomas Jefferson, who had returned from France and taken up the role of the United States' first secretary of state.

By August 1790, at least one matter was solved: Congress had voted to relocate the capital to Philadelphia for ten years until a new city could be built on the Potomac. That city would then become the country's permanent capital. The only thing Congress couldn't come up with was a good name for the new city.

The Adams family moved once again, this time to Bush Hill, overlooking the Schuylkill River in Philadelphia, and Congress moved into the Philadelphia County Courthouse.

Neither John nor Abigail particularly enjoyed living in Philadelphia. It was damp in winter, and even with all the fireplaces blazing, they had to wear overcoats inside on snowy nights. Servants were in short supply, and the ones the Adamses hired were drunk more often than they were sober. Worse, yellow fever raged through the city every summer, killing as many as a hundred people a day.

John was glad to escape to Braintree for the summers. However, the district around Peacefield had been renamed Quincy, after Abigail's grandfather, so John had to get used to saying he was now from Quincy and not Braintree.

In late 1792 the United States held its second presidential election. George Washington agreed to stand for president again, and John Adams, Thomas Jefferson, George Clinton, and Aaron Burr all put their names forward for the election as well.

It was February 1793 before the results were published. They were the same as the previous election. George Washington was reelected president, and John Adams was once again his vice president. This time, though, John knew what to expect of the job. Abigail decided to stay in Quincy, since John could live much more cheaply in Philadelphia boarding with another family, and the three farms they now owned needed a firm hand to watch over them.

John's second term as vice president was overshadowed by the French Revolution. No sooner had John returned to Philadelphia than news arrived that King Louis XVI had been beheaded by guillotine. Blood ran in the streets, and England and Spain declared war on France.

Thousands of Americans pushed for America to come to France's aid, but John saw this as a very dangerous course of action. He wanted America to stay out of foreign wars, and he used all his energy and persuasive powers to see that happen. Meanwhile things in France grew worse, and 1793 became known as the "Reign of Terror." Many of the people John and Abigail had known during their stay in France were among the fourteen thousand people killed as the revolution turned on itself and even many of those who had helped start it were executed.

The war spilled over onto the American continent when France plotted an attack on the Spanish territory of Louisiana, while the British routinely seized American ships crossing the Atlantic, stealing their cargoes and impressing the crews into the military.

The following year, 1794, Congress elected John Quincy Adams as minister to the Netherlands. He was an obvious choice, since he had traveled in diplomatic circles since he was nine years old and he spoke Dutch. Still, many people accused John of securing the job for his son. The charge was not true, but by now John had been criticized and accused of so many things he hardly noticed.

After serving a stormy second term as president, Washington announced he would not run for reelection and was retiring to his plantation in Virginia. This left two likely candidates to succeed him: John Adams, a Federalist, and Thomas Jefferson, an Anti-Federalist, or Republican, as they now called themselves.

The election was bitter and complicated. Jefferson's supporters said all sorts of ugly things about John, and John's supporters did the same with Jefferson. It was a strange moment when the votes were tallied and John found himself the second president of the United States, with Thomas Jefferson, now an ardent opponent, serving as his vice president.

Chapter 16

President

The day of the inauguration was March 4, 1797. That morning sixty-one-year-old John Adams felt queasy. He had lain awake all night worrying about making a mistake during the ceremony, not to mention fretting about the huge responsibility that was about to fall on his shoulders. John wished that Abigail or some other member of his family could be there to give him moral support, but they were all tied up with their own affairs.

John need not have worried about making a mistake because during the ceremony all eyes were fixed on George Washington. Many members of Congress wept openly as they witnessed the last moments of their hero's political career. As he took the oath of office and gave a short speech, John tried not to think of the pitfalls in his path. Washington had been a wildly popular figure, while John was painfully aware that he had won the presidency by just three votes. He knew that Congress would never embrace him as their leader in the same way they had embraced Washington.

When the ceremony was over, John glanced at Washington. He imagined that the former president was thinking, *I am fairly out, and you are fairly in. See which of us will be happier!* John had no doubt that Washington would be the happier of the two and that he himself would have preferred to be at Peacefield. But he was honor bound to do his best to guide the United States through the crisis in Europe.

It did not take long for that crisis to consume both the president and Congress. Just nine days after his inauguration, John received the stunning news that the new French government, which called itself the Directory, had ordered the new United States ambassador off French soil. Furthermore, France had started seizing American ships in the Caribbean, launching a kind of undeclared war. How long John could keep it from becoming an all-out war he did not know.

John also had another, more personal worry. Congress had refused to raise his salary, which remained exactly the same as it had for the past eight years. Costs in Philadelphia had gone up considerably during the time the government had been meeting there, and John was finding it hard to make ends meet. George Washington was a very wealthy plantation owner who had supplemented his presidential income with his own money. But John did not have the spare cash to do this. It was obvious that he could not live the way President Washington had—at least not without a pay raise.

Two weeks after his inauguration, John moved into the presidential house, a large brick mansion on Market Street. Although Washington had left a few items of furniture in the house for John, the servants had held a drunken party and in the process had smashed most of the furniture. John wrote home begging Abigail to wind up their affairs in Quincy as soon as possible and join him in Philadelphia; he needed her to select new furniture and manage the house. The state of Rhode Island had sent John a 110-pound cheese as an inauguration gift, and John wrote that soon this might be all he had left to eat!

Difficulties finding a suitable family to look after Peacefield, along with unseasonably cold weather, had kept Abigail in Quincy. And on April 26, the day before she planned to set out for Philadelphia, John's eighty-eight-year-old mother, who had been sickly for some time, died. By the time John received the letter informing him of her death, the funeral was over. John waited anxiously in Philadelphia for Abigail to join him and tell him all the details of the sad event.

When Abigail finally did arrive on May 10, 1797, she had other difficult family news to tell him. She had stopped off in East Chester to visit Nabby and was distressed at the situation she found their daughter in. Nabby's husband, Colonel

William Smith, seemed to go from one bad land deal to the next. Nabby and the children, who now numbered four, were living a joyless existence in a small town. William often left his family alone for weeks at a time, refusing to say where he was going or what he was up to.

In the meantime, Charles, John and Abigail's middle son, had married William Smith's sister Sally. John hoped Sally was of stronger and more stable character than her brother.

The household shaped up quickly under Abigail's efficient eye, and she took on the role of first lady. John fell into his old habit of getting up at five o'clock in the morning and reading until Abigail joined him for breakfast at eight. Then he went to work, coming home at three for dinner. He rode his horse whenever possible and often took long walks for exercise and to clear his head.

The political news continued to become more ominous. By April 1798 the French had captured more than three hundred American ships trading in the Caribbean and had the audacity to torture the American captains. And in Europe a young, ruthless man, General Napoleon Bonaparte, had taken control of the French military. With surprising ease his army had swept across Italy and Austria and on as far as Egypt. It appeared that he intended to conquer the entire world in the name of France. When the American people heard of these events, they clamored for war with France, but John had seen one war. War held no glamour for him, and he worked harder than ever to bring peace.

Finally French Foreign Minister Charles Maurice Talleyrand agreed to secretly negotiate with American representatives through three of his agents, who came to be known as X, Y, and Z. These secret agents told the Americans that France was ready to make peace with them—for a price. Talleyrand wanted to be given $250,000 for his own use (he did not like to use the word *bribe*), and he wanted the United States to loan the Republic of France ten million dollars!

The American people were outraged when they heard how the French were trying to extort money from the United States, and they wanted war now more than ever. John, however, pursued a course that many could not understand—he continued to work for peace, yet at the same time he prepared for war. He asked Washington to become commander in chief of a new United States army. He also set about creating a permanent navy and signed into law four measures—collectively known as the Alien and Sedition Acts—that Congress had passed. These four measures were a naturalization act that changed the period of residency from five to fourteen years before a person could become an American citizen, an alien act that gave the president power to deport those aliens he judged to be dangerous to the peace and safety of the United States, an alien enemies act that allowed for subjects of an enemy nation to be deported or imprisoned during wartime, and a sedition act that proscribed heavy penalties for conspiracy against the government or for interfering with its operation.

While aspects of the Alien and Sedition Acts seemed to contradict parts of the Constitution, John thought they were necessary in case of war, and it seemed more and more that the United States was tilting toward all-out war with France. And since more than twenty-five thousand French immigrants now lived in the United States, John hoped that these acts would discourage them from becoming agents for France should war break out.

John's signing of the Alien and Sedition Acts would later haunt him. Although Washington privately voiced his support for the acts, Jefferson and the Republicans bitterly opposed them. So too did many Americans. After all, many of them were immigrants who had recently arrived in the country, and the acts directly affected them. But as 1799 rolled around, the rancorous debate over the Alien and Sedition Acts began to die down, and people started to look toward the dawning of a new century.

As the new century approached, one death overshadowed John Adams's presidency and the entire nation. On December 14, 1799, George Washington died after coming down with a cold. The country was plunged into mourning. Pulpits and windows were draped in black fabric, muffled church bells rang out, and stunned people everywhere gathered to comfort each other and wonder how the country would go on without its most beloved citizen. In Philadelphia John and Abigail attended a four-and-one-half-hour memorial service and afterward hosted several hundred people who crowded into their home.

Amid the mourning, the new century approached, and in February 1800 Congress received word that the French Revolution was over. Napoleon Bonaparte had declared himself the first consul and sovereign ruler of France and its vast empire. John's worst fears had come true. The revolution in France had produced not a democracy, as it had in the United States, but a dictatorship led by a power-hungry man.

John knew that the year 1800 would be a significant one for him. It was election year, and the president and vice president were running against each other. John Adams and Thomas Jefferson had not conferred much in the three and one-half years John had been president, and now they hardly spoke to each other at all. Their followers turned the election into a nasty match, with newspapers printing all sorts of accusations and rumors. Among other things, it was said that Jefferson still had French sympathies and that he would ban Bibles if he became president, which would surely start a civil war. John was portrayed as being a weak old man on the verge of insanity who could not even rule his own family.

This last accusation stung John the hardest. It came only months after he discovered that his second son, Charles, was in terrible trouble. Charles had made some bad business deals and gone bankrupt. Instead of facing his problems head-on, Charles had left his wife and two young daughters and taken to a life of drinking. And Nabby's husband, William Smith, was not much better.

Meanwhile John Quincy had married a half-English/half-American woman in London. Of course John's enemies forgot the "half-American" part and accused John and his family of being secretly in love with the British monarchy.

Development of the new capital city, which was now being called Washington, had been going on since 1795, and now the new president's house was supposedly completed enough for the Adamses to move in. They made the move in November 1800.

Washington, D.C., was barely more than a village. None of the new federal buildings were yet complete, the new Capitol was only half built, and as winter approached, the whole place looked more like a mud bowl than a new capital city.

On the second night in the new president's house, which was located on a rise overlooking the Potomac River and the village of Alexandria, Virginia, on the far bank, John sat and wrote a letter by candlelight. He concluded it with the words: "I pray heaven to bestow the best of blessings on this house, and on all that shall hereafter inhabit it. May none but honest and wise men ever rule under this roof."

As 1800 drew to a close, John's mood went from jubilation to despair. On November 3 he had heard the wonderful news that the tensions between France and the United States had been settled. The Convention of Mortefontaine was signed, ending the threat of war with America. Though John was quite certain that Jefferson would defeat him in the coming election, he took great pride in knowing that his steady hand as president had saved America from involvement in a bloody confrontation.

But terrible news arrived less than a month later. Thirty-one-year-old Charles had died of liver failure, the result of drinking too much alcohol. He left behind his widow, Sally, and two young daughters. The older daughter, Susanna, came to stay with John and Abigail at the president's house, while Sally and her younger daughter, Abbe, returned to live with Sally's mother.

It was a shocking personal blow to John and Abigail, who wondered how their gregarious, charming son could have come to such ruin. It appeared that Charles had followed the path of Abigail's brother to personal disaster.

The struggle for the presidency continued, but John had lost some of his fight. On December 3 the electors gathered to cast their votes for a new president. When the results were announced several days later, John was not surprised to have come in third. What surprised him, and a lot of other people, was that Jefferson was not the winner. He and fellow Republican Aaron Burr had tied for first place. The vote tallies were Jefferson 73, Burr 73, Adams 65, and Pinckney 63. According to the constitution, it was up to the House of Representatives to decide whether Jefferson or Burr would be the next president.

The nation had to wait until February 17, when the House of Representatives finally reached agreement. It had taken six days of political maneuvers and thirty-six ballots before the outcome was certain. Thomas Jefferson would be the third president of the United States, and Aaron Burr would be his vice president.

Jefferson's inauguration was set for March 4, 1801, and John had to be out of the president's house by then. As the first president who had ever been defeated, John had no road map to follow in how to act. He decided it would be better if he did not attend the inauguration but rather leave Jefferson and his supporters to celebrate together.

At four o'clock in the morning on Wednesday, March 4, John quietly left the president's house and his position as president of the United States of America behind him. Eight hours later, as John's carriage rolled through the wintry countryside on the way back to Quincy, Thomas Jefferson was officially sworn in as president. At that instant, John went from being the most important man in the land to being a private citizen looking forward to planting his spring crops.

Chapter 17

Independence Forever

John had talked of retirement for years, but when he actually did retire, it was not as rewarding as he had imagined it would be. He had plenty of work to do on the farm but had nothing to do with politics, the career that had passionately absorbed him for nearly forty years. During his first year at home, John was tired and listless and did not even venture as far afield as Boston. Gradually, though, he adjusted to retirement. Books began to beckon him once again, and he started making plans to realign some of the fields on his farm.

John's children continued to bring him great pleasure, and sometimes pain. In September 1801, John Quincy, his wife, Louisa, and their infant son, George Washington Adams, returned from Europe. John and Abigail were delighted to see them again;

it had been seven years since they were last together. John Quincy set up a law business in Boston, and in 1802 he was elected to the Massachusetts Senate. In 1803, at age thirty-five, he became a United States senator. That same summer, Louisa bore a new son, whom they named John, after his grandfather.

John bubbled over with pride at both his new grandson and his son's election to the Senate. He wrote long letters to John Quincy telling him how to behave in various situations.

In truth, it was John's youngest son, Thomas, who needed this kind of advice. As his brother Charles had done before him, Thomas turned to alcohol in an attempt to soothe his disappointments in life. Faced with the fact that his son was an alcoholic, John tried to help as much as he could.

Quincy, Massachusetts, was a backwater compared to Philadelphia, New York, or Boston, but news from Washington eventually found its way there. In 1803 John followed reports of President Jefferson's purchase of the Louisiana territory from France. John Quincy had been a firm supporter of the project.

John also read the shocking news of how on July 11, 1804, Vice President Aaron Burr had dueled with Alexander Hamilton on the banks of the Hudson River. Burr shot Hamilton, who died the following day. Not surprisingly, in the election of 1804, Burr was not a candidate for vice president. Congress had also put in place new rules that said the president and vice president must belong to the same party. Jefferson was elected to a second term as president, and this time George Clinton was his vice president.

Four years later, in the election of 1808, John Quincy did not win a nomination, though the new president, James Madison, appointed him minister to Russia. With heavy hearts John and Abigail bade farewell to their son and daughter-in-law and the couple's third son, two-year-old Charles Francis. The other two boys, eight-year-old George and five-year-old John, remained with their grandparents in Quincy. The departure of his son reminded John of the time thirty years before when he and John Quincy had set out on the dangerous winter voyage across the Atlantic to secure French recognition for his struggling new nation.

Soon after John Quincy's departure, a new addition was welcomed to the Adams family. Thomas Adams married Ann Harrod and moved into the old house at the bottom of Penn's Hill, where John had been born. Ann was a sensible young woman, and John hoped she would help Thomas stay away from drinking.

But there were losses too. Richard Cranch, one of John's oldest and dearest friends, and Mary Cranch, Abigail's sister, died two days apart in October 1810. They were both buried on the same day, and John and Abigail were devastated by the double loss.

By 1812 twelve years had passed since John Adams and Thomas Jefferson had parted ways over the election of 1800. Neither man had spoken to the other since then, and John decided it was time to end the silence between them. He hated to be on poor terms with anyone, and he had such good memories of Jefferson and his family that he wrote him a letter to tell him so.

Much to John's delight, Jefferson wrote straight back, and a lively correspondence grew between them. Sometimes John wrote as many as three letters a week to Jefferson, carefully avoiding politics in favor of such topics as the books he had been reading or some new idea of philosophy he had been thinking about. They often exchanged book recommendations, and John's library soon grew to thirty-two hundred volumes.

In August 1813 John had sad news to report in a letter to Thomas Jefferson. Nabby had come home to die. At forty-eight years of age she was riddled with cancer and had only a few days left to live. Ironically, as she lay dying, her husband, Colonel William Smith, was actually succeeding at something. After being imprisoned twice, once for unpaid debts and once for his part in a mad scheme to liberate Venezuela from the Spanish, he had been elected a congressman for New York.

In 1812 the uneasy peace with Britain had been broken as the two countries had gone to war against each other. A number of small skirmishes had taken place over the next two years, but no decisive battles had been fought. Then, in August 1814, the British assaulted Washington. John was stunned to learn that they had set the president's house and the Capitol ablaze. Neither building was completely destroyed, however, and both could be repaired.

John Quincy was appointed a peace envoy to help settle the war with Great Britain, just as his father had been a peace envoy in Paris in 1782. And just as his father had, John Quincy played an important part in the peace negotiations. On Christmas Eve, 1814, John Quincy and the other American representatives signed a peace treaty with England. The United States was at peace once more.

The signing of the peace treaty did not mean that John Quincy and Louisa would be coming home, as John and Abigail supposed they would. In another strange coincidence, John Quincy was named minister to England, just as his father had been thirty years before. Because John Quincy did not know when he would now be home, he sent word to John and Abigail asking them to send his two sons to England. John and Abigail were reluctant to part with the two active young boys, but they found passage for them across the Atlantic Ocean and escorts to go with them.

Still, it was hard for John to feel lonely after the boys left. Louisa Smith, Abigail's niece, now lived with them, as did Sally Adams and her two daughters, Susanna and Abbe. And Thomas and Ann were producing grandchildren at a rapid rate. While John and Abigail delighted in their new grandchildren, during 1815 some of the people dearest to them died. They included Abigail's sister Elizabeth and her uncle, Cotton Tufts, who had been a faithful helper to the family over the years.

Colonel William Smith died unexpectedly too, leaving the responsibility for Nabby's four children to John and Abigail.

Through all the changes in their family circumstances, John and Abigail took a lively interest in politics. President Madison retired after two terms, as had Washington and Jefferson before him. John supported James Monroe for the presidency in the upcoming election. Monroe won the election of 1816 and immediately asked John Quincy Adams to come home from Europe and take up the position of secretary of state.

This new appointment made John extremely proud. He had set his son on a political course when he was nine years old, and now it was paying dividends. He began to wonder whether John Quincy might one day become an American president as well.

The family had a wonderful reunion, after which John Quincy and Louisa set off for Washington, leaving their children once again under John and Abigail's supervision. George was enrolled in Harvard, and the two younger children were attending a Latin school in Boston. John was now eighty years old and Abigail seventy-two, but they did not see this as a burden. Both of them loved to have their children and grandchildren around, as if they were making up for all the times when the family had been scattered during their lives.

In the fall of 1818 typhoid fever swept through Quincy, and Abigail fell ill with it. Neighbors, friends, and relatives nursed her around the clock. On October 25, their fifty-fourth wedding anniversary, Abigail appeared to be recovering. John was jubilant, but three days later she took a sudden turn for the worse. On October 28, 1818, John stood shaking uncontrollably as he watched his wife's breathing grow weaker. Finally, at midday, it stopped. Seventy-four-year-old Abigail was dead. John gazed at his wife's lifeless form and said, "I wish I could lie down beside her and die too."

Word spread quickly of Abigail's passing, and within hours the entire town of Quincy was wearing black clothes or a black armband. Two days later, no one marked John's eighty-third birthday; everyone was too busy preparing for a funeral the following day.

Abigail's funeral was both simple and dignified, just the way John felt she would have wanted it. John kept up a brave front during the service, thanking those who had traveled from Boston and farther afield to attend. But inside John felt lost; his partner of fifty-four years was gone for good. No one had known him better or loved him more than Abigail.

Abigail's niece continued to live with John and help him with the running of the farms. John was feeling his age now. His hands often shook, his teeth had all fallen out, and he often needed a walking stick to get around, but his mind was as sharp as ever. He still loved to write letters to Thomas Jefferson and the few others of his era who were still alive.

His younger brother Peter died in 1823 at eighty-five years of age, leaving John the only surviving family member of his generation. The house, the fields, Quincy, and Braintree were filled with the memories of John's friends and family. John thought back to his childhood, when he had loved to cut class and hunt in the salt marshes, and to the day he rode to Harvard to take the entrance exam. He pictured his mother waiting at the door for him to come over the hill and his father harvesting corn in the fields. Such memories were all so old now, but they were still vivid in John's mind.

But John still had one more thing to live for. John Quincy was running against Andrew Jackson for president of the United States in the 1824 election. It was a close race, and once again the election resulted in a tie between the two candidates. The House of Representatives had to take a vote, and on February 14, 1825, word reached John that he was now the father of a president. Tears of joy rolled down John's cheeks when he heard the news. He wished Abigail could have been there with him to celebrate their son's election as the sixth president of the United States. It was out of the question for John to travel to Washington for his son's inauguration. He was too old for that, but he held an open house in Quincy that day.

The election had kept John occupied, but once it was over, his health began a steady decline. His eyesight failed, and he felt the strength draining out of him. But just as he had done so many times before, John set himself a goal. He would live to celebrate the United States' fiftieth anniversary on July 4, 1826. Fewer letters now passed between John and Thomas Jefferson, so John had no way of knowing that eighty-three-year-old Jefferson was also ailing and that strangely he had set himself the same goal.

John was invited to attend the huge celebration being held in Quincy for the anniversary, but he was too ill to go. When one of the organizers visited him on July 1, 1826, and asked if he would provide a toast for them to say, John could think of two words that were fitting enough: "I will give you '*Independence Forever!*'"

"Do you have anything to add to that?" the visitor asked.

"Not a word!" John replied.

John fought to stay alive for the next three days, until the dawn of July 4. He listened to the church bells chime and then lapsed into unconsciousness. Around noon he woke up and uttered the words, "Thomas Jefferson survives." He then sank back into a coma.

Many friends and relatives tiptoed into his room as the Fourth of July celebrations went on a little over a mile from Peacefield. Just before the clock struck six in the evening, ninety-year-old John Adams breathed his last and died.

The largest funeral in Quincy's history was held three days later. Over four thousand state officials, Harvard professors, relatives, and neighbors gathered outside the First Congregational Church. There was no way they could all fit inside, and those who could not get a seat waited respectfully as Pastor Whitney preached a half-hour sermon. He chose for his text the Old Testament account of King David's death. "He died in good old age, full of days, riches and honor; and Solomon his son reigned in his stead."

John was laid to rest beside Abigail and Nabby in the churchyard.

Five days later stunning news arrived in Quincy. Thomas Jefferson had also died on July 4, 1826, at the very time John had awakened from his coma and uttered his friend's name.

Americans marveled that two of their presidents, both champions of independence and signers of the Declaration of Independence, had died on the fiftieth anniversary of the great event. The country plunged into mourning unlike anything seen since George Washington had died twenty-seven years before. Cities and towns throughout the United States held memorial parades, some of them with twenty thousand or more mourners in attendance, come to mourn the passing of two great patriots.

Bibliography

Bober, Natalie S., *Abigail Adams: Witness to a Revolution*, Aladdin Paperbacks, 1995.

Ferling, John, *John Adams: A Life*, University of Tennessee Press, 1992.

McCullough, David, *John Adams*, Simon & Schuster, 2001.

Russell, Francis, *Adams: An American Dynasty*, American Heritage Press, 1976.

Shepherd, Jack, *The Adams Chronicles*, Little, Brown, 1975.

Stiles, T. J. (ed.), *Founding Fathers: In Their Own Words*, Berkeley Publishing Group, 1999.

Withey, Lynne, *Dearest Friend: A Life of Abigail Adams*, Simon & Schuster, 2001.

About the Authors

Janet and Geoff Benge are a husband and wife writing team with more than thirty years of writing experience. Janet is a former elementary school teacher. Geoff holds a degree in history. Originally from New Zealand, the Benges spent ten years serving with Youth With A Mission. They have two daughters, Laura and Shannon, and an adopted son, Lito. They make their home in the Orlando, Florida, area.

Also from Janet and Geoff Benge...

More adventure-filled biographies for ages 10 to 100!

Gladys Aylward: The Adventure of a Lifetime • *978-1-57658-019-6*
Nate Saint: On a Wing and a Prayer • *978-1-57658-017-2*
Hudson Taylor: Deep in the Heart of China • *978-1-57658-016-5*
Amy Carmichael: Rescuer of Precious Gems • *978-1-57658-018-9*
Eric Liddell: Something Greater Than Gold • *978-1-57658-137-7*
Corrie ten Boom: Keeper of the Angels' Den • *978-1-57658-136-0*
William Carey: Obliged to Go • *978-1-57658-147-6*
George Müller: Guardian of Bristol's Orphans • *978-1-57658-145-2*
Jim Elliot: One Great Purpose • *978-1-57658-146-9*
Mary Slessor: Forward into Calabar • *978-1-57658-148-3*
David Livingstone: Africa's Trailblazer • *978-1-57658-153-7*
Betty Greene: Wings to Serve • *978-1-57658-152-0*
Adoniram Judson: Bound for Burma • *978-1-57658-161-2*
Cameron Townsend: Good News in Every Language • *978-1-57658-164-3*
Jonathan Goforth: An Open Door in China • *978-1-57658-174-2*
Lottie Moon: Giving Her All for China • *978-1-57658-188-9*
John Williams: Messenger of Peace • *978-1-57658-256-5*
William Booth: Soup, Soap, and Salvation • *978-1-57658-258-9*
Rowland Bingham: Into Africa's Interior • *978-1-57658-282-4*
Ida Scudder: Healing Bodies, Touching Hearts • *978-1-57658-285-5*
Wilfred Grenfell: Fisher of Men • *978-1-57658-292-3*
Lillian Trasher: The Greatest Wonder in Egypt • *978-1-57658-305-0*
Loren Cunningham: Into All the World • *978-1-57658-199-5*
Florence Young: Mission Accomplished • *978-1-57658-313-5*
Sundar Singh: Footprints Over the Mountains • *978-1-57658-318-0*
C.T. Studd: No Retreat • *978-1-57658-288-6*
Rachel Saint: A Star in the Jungle • *978-1-57658-337-1*
Brother Andrew: God's Secret Agent • *978-1-57658-355-5*
Clarence Jones: Mr. Radio • *978-1-57658-343-2*
Count Zinzendorf: Firstfruit • *978-1-57658-262-6*
John Wesley: The World His Parish • *978-1-57658-382-1*
C. S. Lewis: Master Storyteller • *978-1-57658-385-2*
David Bussau: Facing the World Head-on • *978-1-57658-415-6*
Jacob DeShazer: Forgive Your Enemies • *978-1-57658-475-0*

Isobel Kuhn: On the Roof of the World • 978-1-57658-497-2
Elisabeth Elliot: Joyful Surrender • 978-1-57658-513-9
D. L. Moody: Bringing Souls to Christ • 978-1-57658-552-8
Paul Brand: Helping Hands • 978-1-57658-536-8
Dietrich Bonhoeffer: In the Midst of Wickedness • 978-1-57658-713-3
Francis Asbury: Circuit Rider • 978-1-57658-737-9
Samuel Zwemer: The Burden of Arabia • 978-1-57658-738-6
Klaus-Dieter John: Hope in the Land of the Incas • 978-1-57658-826-2
Mildred Cable: Through the Jade Gate • 978-1-57658-886-4
John Flynn: Into the Never Never • 978-1-57658-898-7
Richard Wurmbrand: Love Your Enemies • 978-1-57658-987-8
Charles Mulli: We Are Family • 978-1-57658-894-9
John Newton: Change of Heart • 978-1-57658-909-0
Helen Roseveare: Mama Luka • 978-1-57658-910-6
Norman Grubb: Mission Builder • 978-1-57658-915-1
Albert Schweitzer: Le Grand Docteur • 978-1-57658-961-8
Frederick Douglass: The Right to dignity • 978-1-62486-151-2

Available in paperback, e-book, and audiobook formats.